# Management Mistakes
A Fable for New Managers

# Management Mistakes

## A Fable For New Managers

Don Wood

authorHOUSE®

*AuthorHouse*™
*1663 Liberty Drive*
*Bloomington, IN 47403*
*www.authorhouse.com*
*Phone: 1-800-839-8640*

*© 2012 Don Wood. All rights reserved.*

*No part of this book may be reproduced, stored in
a retrieval system, or transmitted by any means
without the written permission of the author.*

*Published by AuthorHouse 2/8/2012*

*ISBN: 978-1-4685-4242-4 (sc)*
*ISBN: 978-1-4685-4243-1 (e)*

*Library of Congress Control Number: 2012900523*

*Any people depicted in stock imagery provided by Thinkstock are models,
and such images are being used for illustrative purposes only.
Certain stock imagery © Thinkstock.*

*This book is printed on acid-free paper.*

*Because of the dynamic nature of the Internet, any web addresses or
links contained in this book may have changed since publication and
may no longer be valid. The views expressed in this work are solely those
of the author and do not necessarily reflect the views of the publisher,
and the publisher hereby disclaims any responsibility for them.*

# Contents

| | |
|---|---|
| Mistakes | vii |
| Foreword | xi |
| Acknowledgments | xiii |
| Chapter 1 | 1 |
| Chapter 2 | 5 |
| Chapter 3 | 7 |
| Chapter 4 | 10 |
| Chapter 5 | 16 |
| Chapter 6 | 18 |
| Chapter 7 | 19 |
| Chapter 8 | 23 |
| Chapter 9 | 27 |
| Chapter 10 | 31 |
| Chapter 11 | 37 |
| Chapter 12 | 44 |
| Chapter 13 | 48 |
| Chapter 14 | 53 |
| Chapter 15 | 56 |
| Chapter 16 | 58 |
| Chapter 17 | 59 |
| Chapter 18 | 62 |
| Chapter 19 | 65 |
| Chapter 20 | 67 |
| Chapter 21 | 69 |
| Chapter 22 | 72 |
| Chapter 23 | 75 |
| Chapter 24 | 77 |
| Chapter 25 | 81 |
| Chapter 26 | 83 |

| | |
|---|---:|
| Chapter 27 | 86 |
| Chapter 28 | 89 |
| Chapter 29 | 91 |
| Chapter 30 | 93 |
| Chapter 31 | 95 |
| Chapter 32 | 97 |
| Chapter 33 | 98 |
| Appendix A | 100 |
| Appendix B | 140 |
| The Final Word | 145 |

# Mistakes

1. **THINKING YOU CAN DO IT ALL AND NOT SEEKING HELP**

2. **BELIEVEING THAT YOU CAN CHANGE EVERYTHING QUICKLY**

3. **NOT BEING PREPARED FOR MEETINGS WHEN YOU ARE IN CHARGE**

4. **FORGETTING THAT FAMILY COMES FIRST**

5. **REVIEWING PERSONNEL FILES BEFORE YOU HAVE A CHANCE TO DRAW YOUR OWN CONCLUSIONS ABOUT PEOPLE**

6. **NOT UNDERSTANDING THAT ONCE PROMOTED RELATIONSHIPS CHANGE**

7. **NOT MAINTAINING CONTROL**

8. NOT CHOOSING A GOOD ASSISTANT AND NOT TREATING THAT ASSISTANT AS AN IMPORTANT PARTNER

9. READY, FIRE, AIM

10. NOT SEEING INTERNAL AUDITING AS AN ALLY

11. NOT SETTING A BASELINE FOR EVERYTHING

12. NOT ADDRESSING INAPPROPRIATE BEHAVIOR IMMEDIATELY

13. NOT APOLOGIZING WHEN YOU MAKE A MISTAKE

14. NOT PROPERLY DOCUMENTING CONVERSATIONS ABOUT PERFORMANCE AND BEHAVIOR

15. TALKING MORE THAN YOU LISTEN

16. NOT CREATING AND ARTICULATING A VISION OF THE FUTURE

17. SHARING CONFIDENTIAL INFORMATION OR INAPPROPRIATE REMARKS ABOUT YOUR EMPLOYEES WITH OTHERS

18. FAILURE TO UNDERSTAND THAT YOU WILL MAKE MISTAKES

19. NOT INFORMING THE APPROPRIATE PEOPLE WHEN YOU DO MAKE A MISTAKE

20. **THINKING THAT INTEGRITY IS A FLEXIBLE CONCEPT**

21. **ASSUMING THAT EVERYONE IS ENGAGED THE SUCCESS OF THE TEAM**

22. **TREATING TOP PERFORMERS LIKE EVERYONE ELSE**

23. **NOT UNDERSTANDING THE RELATIONSHIP BETWEEN STRATEGY, TACTICS, AND EXECUTION**

24. **NOT UNDERSTANDING THE CRITICAL ISSUES AFFECTING PERFORMANCE AND NOT ENSURING THAT YOUR TEAM UNDERSTANDS THEM AS WELL**

25. **THINKING THAT MEMBERS OF THE TEAM ARE CONCERNED ABOUT YOUR SUCCESS**

26. **NOT USING DATA TO MANAGE**

27. **MICRO MANAGING**

28. **BEING TOO BUSY TO LISTEN INTENTLY**

29. **BELIEVING THAT YOU CANNOT SAY "I DON'T KNOW**

30. **NOT TAKING THE TIME TO HIRE THE RIGHT PEOPLE**

31. **NOT REGULARLY KEEPING THE TEAM FOCUSED ON RESULTS**

32. NOT UNDERSTANDING WHAT MOTIVATES EACH INDIVIDUAL

33. SWEATING THE SMALL STUFF WHILE MISSING THE IMPORTANT THINGS

34. NOT GIVING YOUR PEOPLE THE CREDIT FOR EVERY SUCCESS

# **Foreword**

New managers make mistakes. Managing others is a challenging job; the stress level is high, companies do a horrible job of guiding and supporting new managers and the opportunity to make mistakes is always present.

Why don't experienced managers share their mistakes with new managers? Maybe they don't have time; maybe it never occurred to them. I don't know. Even mentoring program participants shy away from sharing their failures with their mentees. I suspect that they believe that sharing their mistakes is a sign of weakness, since most companies penalize employees for failure.

Who we are is a result of our experiences—good and bad—but we are also a product of our mistakes and successes. If this book can help a new manager avoid some of those mistakes, I have been successful.

Good luck.

# Acknowledgments

Over forty-two years of managing others, I have had the opportunity to come into contact with hundreds of individuals, all of whom have influenced my life. We are all products of our life experiences—good and bad. And the good experiences have outweighed the bad, many times over.

Frank Bramble, CEO of Maryland National Bank, showed me how to communicate during a crisis and how to be as sensitive as possible when I make decisions that affect people's lives. Bill Couper was a wonderful role model, managing with a caring but demanding style. Thanks also to Michael Phung and Jim Carter for showing me how top performers succeed, even in trying times. Dr. MaryJo Anderson was someone with whom I could always discuss concepts and theories. Thanks to Harry Gottwals for giving me a management opportunity.

Aileen Crawford, Bonnie Russo, Bonnie Lowrimore, Lee Watts, and Joanne Arsenault always were honest with me as they guided me. Ken Binion at Sterling Savings Bank proved over and over that auditors are partners rather than adversaries. And Bob Weisel at Sterling always asked the right questions.

For forty of those forty-two years, Melissa has supported me as I succeeded and failed. Thanks for being there.

# Chapter 1

Jim sat nervously in Mike's reception room. Trying to look like he was relaxed, he wondered why he had been asked to come to Mike's office at three o'clock on a Friday afternoon. Mike was Walt's supervisor; Jim worked for Walt. Friday afternoons were always busy for Jim as he tried to tie up loose ends in preparation for the weekend; everyone else was preparing for the weekend and many had already left. In the back of his mind, of course, Jim knew that most companies, his included, announced layoffs and reductions on Fridays. He wasn't quite sure why those announcements occurred on Fridays, but he believed it was to give those being let go time to cool down and to reduce any possibility of violence.

At thirty-two, Jim had been married four years, and his wife Sarah had just resigned from her job to prepare for the birth of their twins. Life would never be the same. They had had numerous discussions about their finances, done their homework, and things would be okay—providing he had a job!

*How did he get here?* Jim wondered. It certainly wasn't by design. He had gone to college without an idea as to what he wanted to be, and he'd found that he had a real knack for numbers, especially financial numbers. Finance was a solid major, and Jim changed his major to finance with the idea of going to Wall Street. But it just was not to be. Graduating from a small college in the Midwest, even with good grades, does not provide the basis for Wall Street. So, when Jim was offered a position with a large national bank in his hometown, he was excited. *I've done pretty well,* he thought to himself. He had been promoted from a financial analyst position to junior banker to a full commercial banker position in eight years, and his success pleased him immensely.

"Jim, Jim," he heard. It was Mike. "Please come in." Mike was considered to be a fair boss, not really concerned about the personal lives of his employees, but fair, honest, and very straightforward. Mike never had time for small talk, and his conversations were always direct and to the point. He had a reputation for being able to manage up the organization and direct his own career, rather than managing his team for performance.

"Have a seat," said Mike. Once Jim had been seated, Mike got right to the point. "Jim," Mike continued, "as you know the past three or four years have been tough on all of us. The difficult economy, the amount of distressed loans that we have had to deal with, the difficulty of generating earnings, and the constant demand from Wall Street to get our house in order—it has been difficult and not much fun for any of us."

Jim was trying to listen carefully but could not help but feel the increasing uncertainty in his mind. *What would he and Sarah do if he was laid off? How would they survive?* Panic was beginning to set in. *Okay,* he thought, *time to focus on the discussion.*

"Jim, because we are not seeing any improvement in the economy, and therefore our ability to generate earnings

*Management Mistakes*

is challenged, over the past few weeks, the executive management team has been meeting to discuss our plans for moving the company forward. As a result of those meetings, we have decided to restructure the company."

Jim was in full panic mode at this point, waiting for the dreaded "we've eliminated your position" phrase.

Mike continued. "As of this afternoon, your boss, Walt, has been told that he no longer has a position with the company. In addition, Gary, the team leader of the other commercial banking team, located at Harbor Square across town, has also been informed that he is no longer needed. Both of them have been told that their last day with our company was today; they have cleaned out their offices and have left the company. In addition, Keith, Gary's assistant, has also been told that he no longer has a position, and he has left the company."

"Jim," Mike said, "we have been impressed with your work ethic, your knowledge, and how you relate to others since you have been with the company. We believe that you have leadership abilities and would like for you to assume leadership of both teams. It will be your responsibility to determine what the teams look like, who remains and who does not, and the optimum organizational structure. While I am here to help, I can let you know that I have been asked to assume greater responsibility and will be adding another business line to my responsibilities. I will ask Linda, my assistant, to place on our calendars monthly meetings so that we can discuss your thoughts and monitor your progress. It is important for you to understand that we must have increased performance out of these two groups as quickly as possible. I have asked Lydia, our HR representative, to schedule a meeting with you on Monday to discuss your first steps, and I suggest that you think about what those first steps will be over the weekend. Your meeting with her is scheduled for 8 a.m. We will be making the announcement regarding your promotion and the reorganization Monday at 9 a.m. on a conference call, and it will appear on our intranet website right after the call. We are looking forward to your leadership and contributions to the success of our company. Congratulations! Do you have any questions?"

*Do I have any questions?* thought Jim.

"No, Mike. I am excited about the opportunity and appreciate your confidence in me. I know that this will not be easy, but I am certain that our team will succeed and be a contributor to the success of your division and our company."

# Chapter 2

Jim and Sarah sat down for carry-out pizza. He had explained to her the events that had led to his new position. They had discussed his lack of experience and the fact that he had no idea as to what his first steps should be. He had no management experience and was still a bit confused about why the bank would choose him over others who might have leadership experience. Sarah had been positive and believed that it was his innate leadership abilities that his supervisors had seen; Jim wondered if it wasn't his low salary that helped Mike make his expense budget.

*No matter,* Jim thought, *I'm the new boss and that's it.*

Sarah asked, "Do you have anyone with whom you can talk about this? Is there anyone at work who has management experience and can give you some guidance?"

"I can't ask anyone at work," said Jim. "Asking for help is a real sign of weakness in this company."

"What about the HR person that you are going to meet with on Monday, can't she help you?"

"Never," said Jim. "Our HR department is senior management's ears, and they repeat everything. You just cannot trust them to be helpful or keep anyone's confidence."

"How about Bill Sullivan down the street? He is a retired senior manager. We like him. He is very pleasant, and it seems like he has always been helpful whenever you asked him questions."

"That's a great idea! I am going to call him Saturday and see if he is willing to meet with me on Sunday. Thanks, honey!"

### Mistake #1: Thinking you can do it all yourself and not seeking help.

# Chapter 3

Jim sat down while Bill turned off the Sunday football game. Bill was in his mid-sixties and had forty years of management experience in a host of different businesses and industries. He was quiet, very smart, and someone who always listened intently before he talked or made decisions. When he retired, employees who spoke at his retirement dinner told of his demanding nature, his expectations that people meet goals, and that employees always do what is right. He had no tolerance for people who cheated and was never afraid to deal with performance issues. Demanding, smart, fair, and caring were the adjectives most often heard from his employees.

"Bill, thanks for taking time from your Sunday football to talk with me. I really appreciate it," began Jim.

"It is my pleasure, Jim. Why don't you tell me what is on your mind and how I can help you?"

"As I told you when I called you, I am with a large national bank and work in the commercial lending division. Until Friday at 3 p.m., I reported to a guy named Walt. Walt was a nice guy who everyone liked but couldn't seem to get everyone working hard and meeting goals. He had been with the company for quite a while and had a lot of friends in the company. On Friday, our company had a major reorganization. Hundreds of people were laid off, including Walt and the head of the other team located across town. I have now been promoted to manage both teams. My new job starts Monday, and I don't know where to start or what to say. I don't even know most of the people on the other team."

"Well, congratulations," said Bill. "I know that you are excited, and that Sarah is very proud of you."

"Thanks, and yes she is. I was hoping that we could talk about what I should do and how I should do it. Again, I have no idea as to where to start; I have no management experience and did not even take a management course in college!"

Bill thought for a moment. "Managing people is always a difficult challenge, Jim—and I am using the terms *management* and *leading* interchangeably—but please understand that they are not the same thing. I once saw an aeronautical engineer being interviewed on TV, and she was asked what she believed to be the most difficult part of her job. The reporter made a little joke about rocket scientists and such. She replied with a smile that managing people was the biggest challenge that she faced!" Bill chuckled as he thought about his own career and some of the experiences over forty years.

"I tell you what, Jim. If you are interested, we can meet on a regular basis and discuss some of your challenges as you begin your management career. What do you think about every other Sunday at my house, for about an hour? You can bring your two weeks' worth of experiences, ask any questions you might have, I can share my thoughts with you, and we can watch a few minutes of football."

"That would be wonderful, Bill. Are you sure that would be okay with you?"

"Of course," said Bill. "Why don't you ask Sarah if it would be okay with her, and let me know?"

"Great."

"So, while you are here, let's talk about Monday and what that holds for you," said Bill. "Tell me what you expect Monday will bring. Is there anything happening on Monday; are there any meetings planned?"

# Chapter 4

Jim mentioned that the reorganization announcements were to be made at 9 a.m. Monday, that a meeting had already been scheduled between his Human Resources partner and him, and that Mike's additional responsibility would also be announced on Monday morning. He expected Mike to be consumed with his new division issues, as the division was very large and in a great deal of trouble. He told Bill that Mike was not one to spend a great deal of time helping his direct reports manage. This was clearly evident when he scheduled a monthly—rather than weekly—meeting with Jim, knowing that Jim was an untried manager.

Bill listened intently as Jim described the situation, including the fact that members of his own team were disengaged, spent the day surfing the Internet, left early, and looked forward to multiple trips to the coffee shop each day. He explained that their excuse was a poor economy, no demand, and the lack of support from the company and its management.

Once Jim was through with his overview, Bill paused a minute to gather his thoughts.

"Jim, one thing that I learned from my many years

of managing lots of different people in many different organizations is that you can't change everything at once. I'll paraphrase a term that you have probably heard: You can't boil the ocean in a short period of time."

## Mistake #2: Believing that you can change everything quickly.

"It certainly sounds as if you have a number of challenges, and I'll be very honest when I tell you that this is not going to be easy; there will be times when it will not be fun, it will take a lot of work, and you will not be anyone's friend. Every day will not be a fun day. But, if done correctly, you will be able to produce a high-performing team made up of individuals who are engaged in the success of the team and company, and you will look back proudly on this experience. Seeing individuals improve their performance and become proud of themselves is one of the most satisfying experiences that you will have during your managing career."

Bill continued, "We need to talk about two things before you leave today. First, how do you plan to handle your meeting with the HR representative? Second, what are the immediate steps that you are going to take once the 9 a.m. announcements have been made? You can be certain that Gary's team has heard the news, and those on your team have heard the news that both Gary and Walt have been let go. Unless there is a leak within the company, they may not have heard that you will be assuming leadership, but I suggest that you assume that they have heard that rumor."

Jim answered, "I have been thinking about a lot of things since Friday, so let me take your second point first. My plan was to wait until after the call and then have a meeting with the members of the team located with me.

I then planned to call over to the other team and set up a meeting the next day."

Bill interjected, "Have you developed your thoughts around why you are having a meeting and what you plan to say?"

Jim was honest when he stated that he had not spent a great deal of time thinking about the meeting. He acknowledged that having a meeting was what his supervisors had done in the past, so it seemed like the right thing to do.

"In addition," stated Jim, "my plan for the meeting was just to get together and talk about the events and get to know each other."

Bill paused a moment and then responded, "I believe that you are correct in your desire to meet with your new team, get to know them, and have them begin to get to know you. One of the mistakes that I made when I began managing, and a common mistake made by newer managers, is not being totally prepared for meetings. As you gain experience, you will be able to ad-lib in some meetings, although I never recommend going into a meeting that you chair without having prepared carefully. Having an agenda, reviewing the details behind the topics, and thinking about the questions or issues that will be raised is crucial to the success of the meeting, your responses to questions, and your ability to avoid making serious mistakes during the meeting."

## Mistake #3: Not being prepared for meetings when you are in charge.

"So," Bill summed up, "tonight, think about why you are having the meeting, what you want to accomplish, what you plan to say, how long the meeting should last, and what questions might be asked. Being prepared and doing what I call pre-thinking can make the meeting run much more

*Management Mistakes*

smoothly and also help you avoid making comments that you might regret later."

"Do you have any suggestions?" asked Jim.

"Well, let's think for a few minutes about that. Right now, there are two teams separated geographically with different managers who have both been let go. Am I correct?"

"Yes," confirmed Jim.

Bill continued, "Normally, Jim, when working with a new manager, I would ask a lot of questions, hoping to lead that new manager to conclusions on his or her own. But, because of the situation and time constraints, let's see if we can develop steps for you to take on Monday and an agenda for your meeting.

"What do you expect to learn from the HR partner at the eight o'clock meeting?"

Jim wasn't quite sure; Mike had given him no indication, and Jim had only a cursory relationship with the person. He expected to learn a bit more about Walt's dismissal, the expectations of the company, and, he hoped, his new title and salary.

Bill agreed that he would probably learn more about his new title, salary, and what office he was to occupy. Bill reminded Jim that he would probably not learn any more about Gary's and Walt's dismissal, since this related to personnel matters and privacy was of the utmost concern.

"So," Bill said, "let's talk about your steps after the 9 a.m. announcement. My experience would suggest that it will be short call, probably led by Mike. He will announce his new duties, the fact that Gary and Walt have left the company, your promotion, and, most likely, direct everyone to an intranet website or to a memo of sorts for other organizational changes. You can be assured that, as soon as the meeting ends, everyone will be looking to see what changes went on throughout the company, and there will be a lot of conversations and gossip related to all of these changes. People need to vent, so this is fine in the short term. Let them talk. There are a number of phases to any reorganization and this is the 'what about me' phase!"

"When would you think a meeting is in order?"

Jim thought that the next day would be appropriate, and Bill agreed.

Next, Bill asked, "How do you plan to notify everyone of your proposed meeting?"

"I thought that I would just walk around and tell everyone in my office and then call everyone at Harbor Square and ask to meet with them the next morning at 9 a.m."

"Good plan," stated Bill. "Now, let's talk about your agenda. My advice would be to keep your remarks short, acknowledge the changes, tell them that you have not had time to absorb the impact on everyone—on the teams, or on the company. Remind them that the number one focus right now is on their customers, and emphasize that they need to contact each customer before the customers learn the news from some other source. Also, remind them that privacy laws prevent them from discussing any personal information about anyone's position in the company and that you would appreciate their not participating in the rumor mill or in any discussions around why individuals were let go. Assure them that you are excited to be working with such a great group of individuals and are looking forward to being the number one team in the entire organization. Share with them your willingness to have individual conversations about the changes. Tell them that the team will have ongoing conversations as the strategic plans of the company are shared and that in the near future you will be having one-on-one conversations with each of them."

"What if they ask questions?" asked Jim.

"You will most certainly get questions from the group," replied Bill. "Here's my advice on questions at this time: One, do not answer any questions or make any comments regarding anyone or any personnel issue. Two, answer any question that you can truthfully answer, but do not answer questions for which you do not know the answer. Three, there will be a lot of questions around changes—you do not have the answers to these or have not been able to develop an answer, so say, 'I don't know.'"

Jim's head was swimming at this point, and he felt lost, inadequate, and extremely unprepared.

Bill could feel Jim's panic. "Jim," said Bill, "we've covered a lot of things this afternoon, so why don't we stop here. I think that you have a good grasp on how you are going to handle tomorrow with both teams. I suggest that you spend some time tonight putting together a short agenda for the meeting so that you don't get off track. You should also know much more about the company's strategy and expectations of you after your meeting with HR; that will help begin to set a direction for you. Some last pieces of advice: Stick to your agenda for the meeting, a short meeting is fine, you do not need to know all of the answers, and making up answers is by far worse than saying that you don't know. Regarding your meeting with the individual from HR, I suggest that you listen carefully, ask about details regarding you, but refrain from sharing ideas, plans, or tactics. You can always do that later, but let's see what that person has to say. Why don't you call me tomorrow night and let me know how things went?"

## Chapter 5

"Good morning, Jim. I'm Lydia, from HR. We have an appointment this morning."

"Yes, we do. Please come in."

Lydia and Jim talked about the company's restructuring, about the economy, and about the fact that the company was positioning itself for the future by rightsizing.

"So, Jim, Mike has asked me to share with you the challenges that he believes you face and the results that he would like to see."

Jim wondered why Mike was not the one to deliver this message, but he continued to listen.

"You have been promoted because we believe that you have the ability to drive this team to success," Lydia continued. "There are clearly some challenges and we know that you are the right person for the job. Let me share some of those challenges. First, we want the two teams brought together in the same location. I have notified our facilities group to begin that process today. Second, the teams have not performed at the level expected, and the company needs for the new team to be a solid—if not top—performer. Our company is looking to drive earnings as quickly as possible,

*Management Mistakes*

and it is crucial that we see a difference quickly. Third, we will be expecting you to determine the structure of the new team and how many individuals you need. This will not be easy, but I am here to help you; all you need to do is ask. I would like to set up a monthly meeting between the two of us so that I can help you with your plan. I have also alerted our facilities group that you will be moving into Walt's office this week, so they have already started that process. The Harbor Square team will be relocating here, since our lease out there is about to expire. Over the weekend, I boxed all of the personnel files of the Harbor Square team, and they will be delivered to you sometime tomorrow; here are the keys to Walt's credenza where he kept his team's personnel files. I have removed your file and will be delivering it to Mike this afternoon; you can, of course, always request to see it."

Jim and Lydia discussed his promotion, his new salary and incentive program, and other details regarding personal details.

She paused for a moment. "Well, it is almost nine o'clock and it is time for the announcements. Do you mind if we take that call together in your office?"

Once the call ended, Lydia thanked Jim for his time, asked if he had any other questions, reminded him that she was always available although very busy, and said that she would send him a meeting request so that they could schedule their monthly meetings. Jim thanked her for her time and advice. Lydia left Jim by himself.

# Chapter 6

Jim sat down at his desk at home. He and Sarah had just finished dinner, and he was trying to remember what they had! His mind was racing a mile a minute, but he had remembered to ask Sarah how she was doing today. He wanted to make sure that his family remained the most important part of his life, regardless of the challenges at work. Sarah really appreciated his attention, since she knew that he was distracted.

**Mistake #4: Forgetting that family comes first.**

# Chapter 7

The phone rang, and Bill answered.

"Well, Bill, I made it through the day and have now been a manager for half a day!"

Bill laughed and congratulated Jim on making it through the day.

"So, tell me about the announcements, your day, and the meetings."

Jim explained the conference call with Mike and described how it had been concise, to the point, and short. He shared Mike's comments about Walt and Gary leaving the company, Mike's thanks to them for their contributions, and Jim's promotion to a leadership position. Mike had then explained his increased duties and the fact that the change would take a great deal of his time. Mike had ended by stating that he had faith in Jim's ability and he looked forward this new team being the top producing team in the bank. "That was it," said Jim.

"How about your meeting with HR?" asked Bill.

"That was okay. I learned a little bit more about why the reorganization took place and why Gary and Walt lost their jobs."

"Oh?" inquired Bill.

"Yes," said Jim. "Apparently, neither team was meeting its performance goals, and the company is determined to generate earnings. The expectation is that every team in the bank will meet its goals. There was a lot of urgency in her voice, so I imagine everyone is going to be under a lot of pressure. I get to determine the structure, how many people we have, and who we keep and who we let go, if anyone."

"That's great, Jim. Have you thought about where to start?"

"Well, the company has already decided to combine the two teams in my present location and they have already decided that I will move into Walt's office, so I don't have to make those decisions. I'm not sure that everyone will move from Harbor Square; I know that a couple of people can walk to work, and this will force them to commute. On the other hand, it's not like jobs are easy to come by right now, so I'm not sure what will happen but either way, I am going to have to make some decisions."

"And how do you plan to make those decisions, Jim?"

"Lydia is having all of the personnel files moved to my office and has suggested that I review them to get a better understanding of each person."

Jim realized that things had become very quiet over the phone. Bill was not responding as he usually did.

"Okay, Bill. What's wrong?"

"I am just thinking about your last remark. What would be your goal in reviewing the personnel files of each employee?"

Jim responded, "Well, the personnel files contain all of the corporate information on each employee, every annual review, and any issues that might have occurred. I want to develop my perception of each employee."

"So, your perception and understanding of each

*Management Mistakes*

employee would be based on the personnel file; at least in the beginning."

Now Jim was quiet. That was a very interesting question, and he could see where Bill was going with it.

"I do know some of the people right now."

Bill remained quiet waiting for Jim to think through the issue. He wanted Jim to come to his own conclusions.

Jim continued, "Bill, I think I know what you are thinking. If I review all of the personnel files then my perception, at least for the people whom I do not know, will be tainted by what someone perceived of them at a different time in that person's life. I think that I would rather draw my own conclusions. So, trying to think this through, maybe I should meet with everyone one-on-one and then review their personnel file afterward. The fact is that whatever happened in the past is really of no concern to me; I am only interested in how each person performs going forward. I have no idea as to their relationship with their previous manager or what might have been happening in their life; rather I care about performance from today."

## Mistake #5: Reviewing personnel files before you have a chance to draw your own conclusions about people.

"Jim, I think that is a perfect suggestion," Bill said. "As a new manager, the world for you and your new team begins today. Your performance and their performance will be judged based on results going forward—not something that happened a year ago. I think that you have just made your first major management decision. Congratulations! Don't forget that we will be getting together next Sunday for our discussion. How about three o'clock as my Packers beat up on somebody?"

"See you at your house at three o'clock, and thanks a lot, Bill."

# Chapter 8

It was Tuesday morning, and Jim was in his new office early. The meeting with his new team was scheduled for 10 a.m., and he wanted to be prepared for that meeting. First impressions are everything, and he wanted to make a good first impression.

"Good morning," said Derek. Derek was Jim's best friend at work and, up until a few days ago, a peer. They had started about the same time and had become the best of friends. Their wives liked each other, and they had spent vacations during the past two years together. Derek had no management desires or ambitions, so Jim's promotion was not an issue for him. Jim worried a bit, but Derek had assured him on Saturday that he was fine with the change and that he would support Jim in any way possible.

"Ready for the big meeting?"

"I think so," replied Jim. "Just a little nervous."

"I guess," said Derek. "It will be interesting to see how you handle Craig and Alicia today. I know that neither is happy that Walt and Gary were let go, and they have been really vocal about it since Friday."

"I don't know Craig very well, since he was on the other

team, but Alicia is another story! She is so emotional and irrational and just can't keep her mouth shut."

"She could be a problem for you, buddy," said Derek.

"I know; I am not looking forward to dealing with her. She's been nothing but trouble since she got here. All she wants is her way and attention, attention, attention. And she's a poor performer."

"Hey, it's now your problem! Good luck with that," Derek said with his usual cynical tone.

## Mistake #6: Not understanding that once promoted relationships change.

As Derek was leaving, Julie walked in.

"How are you doing, Jim?"

Julie was just a wonderful person and one of the best assistants in the company. While she loved working for Walt, she liked Jim a great deal and was genuinely happy that he had received the promotion. She had been in her position for more than ten years and had seen a number of managers come and go. She and Jim worked well together, and she had made it clear that she would do her best to make sure that he succeeded.

"Are you ready for the meeting? I have the conference room set up. Do you need any computers, overheads, or anything electronic?" she asked.

"No, and thanks for everything," Jim replied.

"All the offices are ready for the Harbor Square team, phones are working, and they all have either their new laptops or are bringing their old ones with them. I will have the paperwork transferring everyone to the new office ready for you to sign this afternoon. Once you sign it, I'll take care of making sure it gets to the right place."

"Thanks again, Julie. You are just amazing. I guess I am a little overwhelmed with everything; anything that I need to know right now?"

Julie sat down. They had about thirty minutes before the meeting started.

"Are you ready for the meeting? Are you sure that you don't need more preparation?"

"Nope; on another topic, is there anything that you can share with me that I might not hear from anyone else?"

"Well, so here is some information that you probably need to know. First, there are some rumors going around that Walt and Gary, being the old boys that they were, did not think that women ought to make as much as the traditional heads of the households—men. That rumor has been around for a long time, and it really grates on the women in both teams. They have been scared to go to HR because HR always shares information with management and it comes back to haunt everyone."

Jim asked, "Do you think that the rumor could be true in this day and time?"

"Don't know," replied Julie "But you need to know that there is a rumor.

"Another rumor going around is that Gary used his expense account for things that the company would not normally approve," Julie went on. "People are saying that, in many cases, he asked others to put the expenses on their reports so that he could approve them, and no one else would ever see them."

"Like what?"

"Well, lunches with no customers, ball games with no customers, even parties at his house where he invited employees," she replied.

"And the last thing that you should know is that neither department has had any type of audit in over three years. I have tried to make sure that we are in compliance with everything, but it is difficult. Both Walt and Gary kept postponing audits, and, for some reason, the audit department kept agreeing. You might want to think about that."

"Thanks so much, Julie. I can't imagine taking this job without having you here and having your support. Would you please call internal auditing and HR and schedule a face-to-face meeting with Lydia and the head of internal auditing?"

## Chapter 9

"Good morning, everyone," Jim said as he entered the conference room. The response was warm but guarded. Jim had not thought about where he would sit, but it was clear that everyone expected him to sit at the head of the long conference room table. Instead, he quickly made the decision to sit in the middle, between Alicia and someone from Harbor Square whom he did not know.

He began, "Thank you for taking time from your schedule to meet today. I want to acknowledge that this is a difficult time with all of the changes that have recently been announced. In the short time since the announcements, I know that all of us have lots of questions but not many answers. I want to share with you high-level information regarding why the company-wide reorganization took place and how that affects us. As was noted in the conference call, the company has been going through a rough period and must change with the changing times. There is an urgency to produce earnings as quickly as possible. That urgency required expense reductions, and we will be hearing more about that over the next few weeks and months. On the other side of the coin, expense reduction never creates revenue. Senior management has expressed confidence in this group and its ability to quickly generate earnings. I know that Mike certainly has high expectations for this team. I wish I could give you more details, but at this point I just don't know any. But, like Mike, I also have a lot of faith in our team's ability to meet its goals and make a significant contribution to the success of our company. I will be asking Julie to set up regular team meetings starting next Tuesday. It seems that, with all the changes, we should be meeting weekly at least in the beginning. Also, I suggest that we meet on Tuesday mornings so that we leave Monday free to plan and organize for the week. Is that okay with everyone?"

There was silence with just a few head nods. Jim took that as agreement.

"Okay," he said. "With that, let me open the floor for comments and questions. Does anyone have any items that he or she would like to discuss?"

Craig spoke up, "Well, I'm not happy with the way things have gone. First of all, the commute is a real pain; I didn't get any extra money for gas, and I have an office that overlooks a parking lot rather than one that overlooks trees. All the company does is think of itself. Gary was a great guy, and we all liked working for him. He was easygoing, did not demand a lot, and knows everyone in town. It is just unfair that he is out of a job. I'll bet if I were a woman, I'd have a nice office."

Everyone looked at Jim. Jim could feel himself getting stiff, and he tried to remain as calm as possible.

"I've been through this stuff before," continued Craig. "It's always the little guys in the company that get shafted; you can bet the people at the top still have their bonuses and perks."

"Actually, Craig, the announcements on the intranet on Friday stated that all senior management bonuses were being stopped for this year and that the top twenty executives were going to take a 10 percent salary cut," said Jim.

"Garbage! They'll find some way to reward themselves for the mess that they put us in. Screw the workers is always the theme. And, I trade an office with a view for an office where I get to count cars. It never ceases to amaze me that the guys at the top always get the rewards. I've worked for seven different companies in the past sixteen years and it is always the same. I can't wait to get to the top," he continued. "It's always the same—ask for more and more from the worker, give more and more to the top, fire the good guys, and promote people who don't know what they are doing."

Craig stopped to take a breath. No one in the room knew if he understood what he had just said, but they did. Everyone in the room looked at Jim.

Jim had reached his tolerance point. "Craig," he said strongly, "I believe that you have said more than enough. It is clear to me and should be clear to everyone else that our senior management team is making sacrifices. The strategic direction of our company is clear, and the requirements of the marketplace and our stockholders should also be very clear to all of us. The fact is that if you and the rest of the company had been spending as much time on reaching goals as you did on complaining, we would not be in this state of affairs. The company does not pay any of us to come to work and enjoy the view outside our window; it does pay us to come to work and produce returns for our stockholders— and that is what we are going to do, starting today."

## Mistake #7: Not maintaining control.

Again, the attendees were quiet.

"Are there any more comments or questions?"

There were none.

Jim ended the meeting by asking Julie to place on everyone's calendar a weekly meeting every Tuesday for the next three months. Jim again thanked everyone for coming to the meeting and stated again that he was proud to be the team leader and excited about working with each one of them.

# Chapter 10

Generally, Jim ate lunch at his desk while he worked, and today was no exception. He was not feeling good about the meeting, and Craig's inability to keep his mouth shut was bothersome. Jim was also concerned about his own comments and outbursts. *Was it too much? What else could he have said? Didn't he need to address Craig's remarks?* He wasn't sure but he had plenty to do.

Five o'clock was approaching just as Lisa peeked in the door. Lisa was a good performer from the Harbor Square team, and, while Jim had met her, he did not know anything about her except that she was consistently the top performer on that team. Gary had always spoken highly of her.

"Hi, Jim, I hope your day has been okay. I just wanted to let you know that I am glad that you are leading our team. I'm also glad that the two teams were finally brought together; some of us have wondered for a long time why that did not happen. I feel that I can learn a lot from some of the others."

"Thanks, Lisa. I appreciate your stopping by and your comments. I can tell you that I am excited about the two teams becoming one, and I am excited about the potential we have as a group."

Lisa responded, "I think it is exciting also, but it is not going to be easy in this economy. We're a team now, so full speed ahead!"

"Thanks again, Lisa."

Lisa turned to leave and then stopped, turning to Jim.

"By the way, Jim, Craig's behavior in the meeting was normal for him. We've learned to not pay attention to him. He doesn't really mean any harm, so don't worry about it. Have a good evening."

"Thanks again," said Jim.

Lisa left just as Julie came into Jim's office.

"I'm getting ready to go but wanted to let you know that I was able to schedule a meeting on Friday with Lydia from HR and Ken, the head of internal auditing. They'll be here at 9 a.m. on Friday. I have scheduled the conference room for you."

"Thanks so much, Julie, I don't know what I would do without you," Jim said warmly.

"We'll make it, Jim. Been there, done that. We'll be fine," said Julie with her usual positive attitude.

"May I ask you a question?"

"Sure."

"I am not feeling very good about the meeting today. I was disappointed with Craig's outburst, especially since it was our first meeting. You were there, and I trust your judgment. What was your impression?"

"I'm not really a good person to ask, Jim. I am just an assistant."

"But, Julie," insisted Jim, "you have been an assistant for many years, and you have seen both managers and employees come and go. You have seen the good and the bad. I am sure that you have an opinion, and I trust your judgment. Also, I need someone who will come to me with honest and candid feedback, tell me when I shouldn't do something, and share with me the honest truth. If I am about to screw up, I need for you to tell me so. That's the relationship that I would like to have between us."

## Mistake #8: Not choosing a good assistant and not treating that assistant as an important partner.

"Okay, I think that we can have that relationship. I have worked for a lot of people and have had that relationship only with a few: Stan, whom you never knew, but you might have heard his name, was the one who relied on me the most to give him feedback. I can do that, and if I ever cross a boundary, you need to let me know."

She continued, "Craig has been like that since he started here. He is a real hothead, and sometimes—well, most of the time—he speaks without thinking. In the beginning, everyone was upset, but as time has progressed, everyone has learned to just ignore him, and the common saying I hear is that's just the way Craig is. I think people still get upset, but probably more embarrassed, by his comments and childish behavior. Sometimes, he really lashes out at those in the room, but most of the time it is all about him. I talked with Gary's assistant regularly, and he was always mentioning Craig's outbursts. There were a number of times when he mentioned that he had really slammed people outside the team and it caused Gary some problems."

"Has anyone ever said anything to him?" questioned Jim.

"Well, I have heard that he and Gary had some closed-door meetings, but nothing seemed to change. You know how Gary was—everything is fine—he hated confrontation.

I suggest that on Friday after you meet with Lydia and Ken, you might want to talk to Lydia about him and see what she has to say."

"That's a great idea, and thanks for sharing that information."

"You're welcome," said Julie as she turned to leave.

"May I ask you one more question while you are here?"

"Sure."

Jim hesitated a bit. "I reacted to Craig's inappropriate comments because it upset me and because I wanted to make sure that he knew that his behavior was inappropriate. Can I get your reaction to my comments?"

"It was fine," said Julie

"That's not exactly rousing support, Julie. Remember, I have asked you to be brutally honest with me in everything, and I would really appreciate your honesty."

"Well, Craig has been doing this a long time, and each time he does it, he either gets his way or he gets everyone in the office riled up. People end up talking about his immature behavior for days and, in most cases, in order to appease him, Gary would give in. So, first, I think that the group is waiting to see if you move him to the open office on the corner, which is what he really wants. Second, he reminds me of a child who throws a tantrum and the parents often overreact. When your twins get to be around two, and until they are four or so, when they want to get their way and can't, they'll throw tantrums. It might be at home, at the grocery store, in front of friends, strangers, or family—it doesn't matter to them. They want their way, and they will do whatever it takes to get it. You are going to have three choices: First, grab them yell, scream, and maybe spank them. Second, ignore them, and third, think about what is going on, act in a way that you are under and in control, and take charge. As a mother, it was really hard not to get in that first mode and really get mad and overreact. As a grandmother, number one is always out. So, I quickly look at the situation and decide whether to just ignore what is happening or react in a controlled manner."

## Mistake #9: Ready, fire, aim.

Jim, realizing that he had asked for the honest feedback, asked, "In what category would you put my reaction?"

"I'm not a psychologist, but, using my mother skills, I think Craig had two purposes for his outburst. First, I think that he wanted to get you to change his office, and second, he wanted to get a reaction out of the group. Focusing on the office and outburst takes away from the focus on Craig and his performance. I would put your reaction in category number one: overreaction."

"What would you have done, Julie? How would you have reacted?"

"Jim, I am not a supervisor, so it's difficult for me to say."

Jim pressed. "Okay, get into your mother mode, and tell me how Julie the mother would have reacted."

Julie chuckled. "I would have thought about Jim's purpose and realized that he was testing me, just like your teenagers will do in thirteen or so years. I feel awkward telling you this."

"Don't," said Jim. "I want honest feedback as I said; we'll get accustomed to being very candid with each other."

"Okay, Craig had an agenda—to get his way and stir the pot. He accomplished his second goal, and you helped him accomplish that by losing control. I am sure that he feels that he got his way again, which will encourage him to try it once more."

"So, what would you have done?" inquired Jim.

"I'm not sure that I am qualified to answer that question," Julie said hesitantly.

Pushing, Jim answered, "Sure you are, you have been an assistant working for a lot of bosses over the years, and, most importantly, you have been the mother of three teenage boys. That ought to qualify you to run the company!"

"I would have either let him finish or, if I felt it was going too far, I would have interrupted. You needed to take control of the situation before it got out of hand. In this case, his rant was short for Craig, so maybe letting him finish would have been okay. I would have said to him that you appreciate his strong feelings; however, in the future you expect everyone in the room to present their concerns in a calm, professional manner, and if anyone has personal issues, they need to be shared with you in a private setting. I would have then moved to the next piece of business on your agenda."

"This has been really helpful; thank you so much for your honesty. Would you do me a favor and schedule a meeting between Craig and me after my meeting with HR and auditing on Friday, and maybe you could make it in the afternoon, since I'll be meeting with Lydia after the meeting with Ken and her?" asked Jim.

"Absolutely," replied Julie.

*Boy, I am glad this day is over,* Jim thought to himself.

# Chapter 11

Thursday came and went, and Jim was able to learn a bit more about where the company was headed. He spent part of Thursday preparing for his meeting with HR and auditing while also thinking about his upcoming meeting with Craig.

"Good morning, Jim," Lydia said as she entered the room. "Am I early?"

"No, right on time," said Jim. "Before Ken gets here, did Julie schedule a meeting between you and me right after this one?"

"Yes, she did, and I have plenty of time."

Ken, the head of internal auditing, entered the room, and everyone introduced themselves.

"Thank you both for making time for me on such short notice and also for coming to my office. I really appreciate the support. Let me get right to the point. As both of you know, I am new to this position and, in fact, have never managed before. So, not only is managing people new to me, everything about administration is also new and, I might add, a bit overwhelming."

Ken added, "Jim, we all know that you are new and

inexperienced. Senior management of this company has a lot of faith in you and believes that you are the right person to make this team successful and lead it to new heights. All of us in support positions are committed to ensuring that we do everything possible to make you successful."

"Thanks, Ken, that's why I asked both of you here today," Jim continued. "This is still my first week in this position, but I have been told that there might be irregularities within both teams."

"What type of irregularities?" asked Lydia.

"Well, I'm not quite sure, but let me tell you what I have heard so that we can discuss and develop a plan."

Jim went on to state that he had heard that there were some expense irregularities, where non-company-related activities had been charged to the bank. He was specific in relating the comments regarding the Harbor Square team, and he admitted that he knew nothing about his former team's expenses.

Ken interrupted, "Jim, my team can do a complete audit of expenses and the controls in place. The company has specific procedures, but sometimes the procedures are not followed or the supervisor is a bit lax. I came from a company where we terminated an individual for buying tires for his sports car using the company's credit card. That was not caught for over two years."

"That's great," stated Jim. "What other areas do you think are important?"

"Well, we are a bank. So, we will come into your area with a full-blown comprehensive audit. We'll look at credit files and expenses, we'll do a fixed asset audit to ensure that stuff just hasn't disappeared, and we'll compare what you team does with our established and written procedures. In addition, we will compare the costs of supplies for your teams to similar teams to see if supplies are disappearing or, at least, being used in excessive amounts. We'll make sure that security procedures are being followed, ensure that third-party vendors are abiding by their contracts—we'll get vendor management to help us—and we'll develop a complete report for you."

"Will this report provide me with recommendations for fixing any issues, improving controls, and maintaining proper audit procedures?"

"Yes, it will, Jim," replied Ken.

"Wow, that's great." Jim was very excited.

Lydia asked, "How can I be of assistance, Jim?"

"You can help me in two ways. First, above everything else, I want to be seen as a fair person. It is important to me that I treat everyone fairly, not necessarily equally, but fairly. I once had a professor whose students described as tough but fair. That seemed like a great compliment to me. Second, we have a lot of diversity on this team and a lot of strong personalities. I don't want to be surprised by things that have happened in the past that I don't know about."

## Mistake #10: Not seeing internal auditing as an ally.

"Can you give me an example of what you are thinking?"

"Gary and Walt were great guys from the old boys club, but I am not confident that they treated everyone the same—especially in salaries. I am also not confident that monitoring compensation equality has been a focus of the HR department. And by equality, I mean whether, taking into account years of service and performance, the salaries among the various groups of individuals are justifiable."

Lydia responded, "So, you would like for us to review the compensation of the individuals on both teams in terms of gender, race, and any other factor that might reflect prejudice on the part of the past supervisors, in order to determine if we can find any evidence of bias?"

"That is exactly what I want," said Jim.

Lydia agreed to provide that for Jim, stating that it would take a couple of weeks to complete. They agreed that, once she had completed the report, she would schedule a meeting to discuss the results.

"This is great," Jim said with enthusiasm. "I appreciate your support and thanks again for coming today."

"May I ask one more question?" Ken asked. "I have been running audit teams for more than twenty years, and I have never had anyone call me and request a thorough internal audit when he or she did not even know if anything was wrong. How did you come to this conclusion?"

"Well," Jim replied, "I have a brother who is an auditor, and we have had a lot of conversations regarding the hostile environment within companies toward auditors. In most companies, the relationship between the auditing teams and the rest of the company is tense at best. I guess, after years of these discussions, I have been convinced that internal auditors have no stake or concern about my success or failure; they have only one focus: Are there controls in place to minimize risk and loss, and is the unit adhering to those controls? I understand that, at times, I will have to make business decisions that increase the risk of loss, but those are business decisions. By having a baseline of where we are, what the policies are, and how we are conforming to those policies, I have a sound basis for making decisions that could increase risk. I am always baffled when I hear people talking about how they hate internal auditors."

## Mistake #11: Not setting a baseline for everything.

*Management Mistakes*

"That's great, Jim. I wish everyone in our company felt that way. My team will be excited to learn about your philosophy, and I can guarantee you that we will do everything that we can possibly do to uncover any issues and make sure that you are successful."

Jim concluded the meeting. "Ken thanks again for all of your support. I have another meeting with Lydia, and I will wait to hear from you as to when your team will be here."

An excited Ken responded, "You bet. I'll be back to you within a week or so. Have a good weekend."

Ken left the room excited about the new relationship and determined to live up to his promise of ensuring that Jim was successful—at least in every area over which Ken had influence.

Jim proceeded to tell Lydia about his first team meeting and Craig's inappropriate comments and behavior. He shared with her his reaction to it and the conversation that he had had afterward with Julie.

"So," said Jim, "Can you tell me a bit about Craig and his previous behavior? I have not reviewed his personnel file to see what is in it."

"You won't find anything in his personnel file, Jim. I came to the company right after Craig, and he was already a legend! He has been throwing tantrums since he arrived, and, in most cases, he has gotten what he wants after the tantrum. Gary was tired of having to deal with personnel problems and did not like any type of confrontation, so, in most cases; he caved in to Craig's demands. Oh, every once in a while he would take Craig into his office and lecture him, but it was gentle, and I believe that Craig probably dominated the conversations."

"I haven't followed Craig's performance since it did not mean anything to me; is he a top performer?"

"Actually, he's not."

"Well, that might explain his job hopping. In his tantrum, he mentioned that he had been with seven companies in sixteen years. Maybe some of them also got tired of his behavior."

Lydia stated defensively, "There was never any documentation by his previous employers that he had a behavior issue. And, in today's world, we never get any information from the employer about performance."

"I understand," said Jim, not wanting to imply that HR had not done its job.

"Here's what I am going to do. I am meeting with Craig this afternoon, and I am going to tell him that his behavior was unacceptable, that I did not appreciate the comments and tone, that I expect him to always act in a professional manner, and that, if this type of behavior happens again, he and I will be discussing his future with the company. And, I need your support and the support of HR on this matter."

## Mistake #12: Not addressing inappropriate behavior immediately.

"I can make myself available to attend if you like," Lydia offered.

Jim thought for a minute. "In this case, I think it would be better for Craig and me to meet alone. As his new manager, I am going to give him one chance to start over and to change; if I involve you, he will not see it as his one chance. I will tell him that, if such an outburst happens again, I will involve HR, and he will be placed on formal warning, according to our company policy."

"Okay," said Lydia.

"By the way, Lydia, why does our company allow such behavior? During my time with this company, I have been amazed at the stories that I have heard about some people's outbursts, tantrums, and comments—and yet these people are still around, some in top level management jobs. It seems to me that if we want to live up to our published statements about being a place where people want to work, where we respect each other, and where integrity is high on our list of priorities, we should have zero tolerance for such behavior. Some of these people have been here for a long time, and the stories go back years and years. I guess I just don't understand why we tolerate such behavior from anyone."

Lydia fumbled for an explanation. "We are working with those individuals."

## Chapter 12

Jim had time before his meeting with Craig, so he tried to relax for a few minutes before he had to prepare for that meeting. He knew that he needed to be well-prepared, clear in his message, and calm.

The knock on the door was the signal that Craig had arrived.

"Good afternoon, Craig," said Jim.

"Hi, Jim." Craig's response was relaxed and showed no hint of concern.

"Please come in, and would you please shut the door?"

Craig shut the door and took a seat across the desk from Jim. Jim had prepared well for the meeting and knew exactly what he wanted to say. The unknown was how Craig would react to the message.

"Craig, I wanted to spend some time this afternoon discussing the meeting on Tuesday and some of the remarks that were made. First, I would like to apologize for my remarks and for the tone of my remarks."

**Mistake #13: Not apologizing when you make a mistake.**

"No problem," said Craig. "I don't even remember what was said."

At that moment, Jim understood what he was dealing with. Here was a guy who threw tantrums because they worked, didn't really realize what he was saying or doing, and quickly moved on to something else. It happened so often that it was just what he did.

"I think it is important for me to express my apology, Craig. It is not my nature or expectation of me to say such things, and I certainly apologize for that."

Jim continued, "The other reason I wanted to meet with you is to talk about your comments and behavior in the meeting. It was unacceptable and unprofessional. Your comments about your office and your comments about women getting preferential treatment were very inappropriate. It was very awkward for everyone in the room and very demeaning to the women in the room."

Craig interrupted, "I didn't even realize that I said anything inappropriate."

Jim continued, "Let me make myself very clear. I do not expect to hear you make inappropriate remarks again, as long as we work together; I do not expect to hear a single demeaning reference to women or any other class of people, as long as we work together; and I expect you to air your grievances with me privately and not with anyone else. Our company has a high standard of integrity and respect for each employee, and we demand that everyone show respect for his or her colleagues. Your inappropriate remarks in the meeting suggest that you do not adhere to those standards. I want to make it very clear that those are the standards of the company, and you can either abide by those standards or choose to leave the company. If you decide to stay, there is no leeway regarding your behavior.

"Two other points need to be made. First, you have

a history of overreaction, some would say tantrums. I understand that these have been going on for years and that, in many instances, you have gotten exactly what you want by acting unprofessionally. Starting today, tantrums, yelling, and unprofessional behavior will not be tolerated. If I see you acting in such a manner or hear about you acting in such a manner, I will take the appropriate action—and that action will be placing you on disciplinary action. If it occurs a second time, that will result in my terminating you from the company. You are an adult and a professional, and you are expected to act as such. Again, I want to make it clear that if this happens again, I will take immediate and strong action. Do I make myself clear about this?"

Craig was stunned. "Yes."

"In addition, Craig, the decisions made regarding office space were made with a number of factors in mind, including time with the company and past performance. You were assigned the office you now occupy and that is your office. You will not be relocated. I do not want that brought up again. Do I make myself clear on that issue?"

"Yes," said Craig.

"Next week, I will be giving you a written summary of this meeting; you are welcome to review it, and if you disagree with the contents, which will reflect what we have talked about, you are welcome to come and talk with me about it. I will be placing a copy of the memo in your personnel file. Again, the memo will be a summary of the facts of our discussion this afternoon."

## Mistake #14: Not properly documenting conversations about performance and behavior.

Jim paused, and Craig just nodded his head in agreement.

"Craig, I appreciate your taking the time to meet with me today, and I am hopeful that you will be a high-performing, valuable, and participating member of our team going forward."

# Chapter 13

The Packers were winning when Jim sat down in Bill's den for their Sunday meeting.

"Bill, it seems like I have been managing for years after this week. I don't know where to begin, but let me try."

Jim explained to Bill the moving of the teams, the meeting, Craig's outbursts, and the manner in which he had dealt with Craig.

Bill interjected, "So, what did you learn?"

"That I need to always maintain control when dealing with issues."

"That's a good lesson to learn, Jim. You can be upset, and you can be angry, but maintaining control is very important. Losing control gives the wrong impression to your folks, and, more importantly, it often results in your saying things that you regret."

Bill continued, "I am impressed with the fact that you dealt with Craig immediately and in a clear fashion. It was important to address that type of behavior quickly. One other point on that—as the senior person in charge, you can be held personally accountable for the actions and comments of your subordinates, so dealing with it immediately and firmly is crucial. Did you inform your HR department of the incident and how you handled it?"

"Yes."

"And did you write a summary of the conversation and place it in his file?"

"I am going to do that this weekend, and I was planning on giving him a copy and asking him to sign that he received a copy. Is that what you would do?"

"It certainly is," replied Bill.

Bill continued, "The other thing that I like, Jim, is that you felt that it was important to apologize for your remarks when you lost control. Too often, managers, both new and experienced, feel that since they are the boss, they don't have to apologize for anything. This not only sets a bad example, it also creates a tone of resentment in the office. Good work.

"So, Jim, what is your plan going forward?" Bill concluded.

"I plan to have my weekly meeting and then I was thinking about meeting with each team member individually to learn about them. I'd like to learn about their goals, strengths, etc."

"Have you thought about those meetings?"

"Not much. Can you give me some guidance as to what they should look like?"

"These meetings give you an opportunity to understand each employee—or at least begin that process. I think that there are a number of important things for you to think about when conducting these meetings. First, you and I have talked about my philosophy toward preparing for meetings. It is, again, crucial in these meetings. So, I would develop a few questions that I would ask all of them to get the discussion started. Second, as a manager, it will be easy for you to do most of the talking—after all, we have all of the answers! This would be a huge mistake. You will learn that it is important to listen intently and to listen a lot more than you talk."

## Mistake #15: Talking more than you listen.

"I found that I learned much more by listening than I did talking. There's an old saying: listen to understand, not to respond."

Jim was listening!

Bill continued, "Tell me about your next all-team meeting. What do you plan to do there?"

Jim thought for a minute. "I haven't really spent much time thinking about it; there are always a lot of corporate things to cover, especially with the reorganization."

Bill went into his lecture mode. "There are two points I need to make here, Jim. Number one is being prepared for the meeting that you run. You and I talked about this earlier, and you will hear me mention this time and time again. It is crucial that you are prepared. I would suggest that you develop a standard agenda that you can use each meeting. By having a standard agenda, you can start on time and stop on time. If you need more time once in a while, you can inform everyone in advance, which allows them to adjust their schedules.

"Number two," Bill continued, "You need to start developing a vision for your group."

"I'm not sure what you mean," responded Jim.

"By developing a vision, you and your team know where you are going and to what end you are striving."

"We have goals," said Jim.

"Vision and goals are not the same. A vision is a look at the future: where do you want to be at a given time? This gives your team an understanding of the direction in which you expect them to go."

"Can you give me an example?" asked Jim.

## Mistake #16: Not creating and articulating a vision of the future.

"Let's see. When Jack Welch took over GE, he stated that GE would be either number one or number two in the world in every business line that GE managed. That statement told everyone to what he was striving for and the direction that he wanted everyone to go."

"So, something like 'we want to meet all of our goals' might be a vision statement?"

Bill corrected Jim and suggested that he think in broader terms. After some discussion, Jim said, "Our team will be the most profitable team in our organization."

Bill commented, "That is a good vision and one that allows your team to understand exactly where it is headed. John Kotter, in his book *A Force for Change,* states that a vision 'is specific enough to provide real guidance to people, but vague enough to encourage initiative and to remain relevant under a variety of conditions.'"

"Once a vision has been determined," Bill continued, "I suggest that you, not your team, create the vision. Only then strategies are developed that will help you reach that vision. You can then establish specific tactics that support the vision and goals that help you to have markers along the way. Again, I suggest that you develop and articulate the vision and then get your team involved in developing strategies and tactics. I also expect that most of your goals are set at the corporate level, so you don't have much leeway with them, although you can set your own goals if the corporate goals don't fully support your vision."

Bill could see Jim's mind working.

"There are a number of other things around visions of which you should be aware," continued Bill. "Some of these are common among all leaders, and you can see them in some of the biggest companies in the world. First, you will fret over the vision and the specific wording. It will become part of you, you will understand it, and you will live it. Don't think that the rest of your team is moving along that road with you. You will need to say it, say it, say it, and then remind them again of the stated vision. Second, I suggest that you get your entire team involved in developing the strategies and tactics that they will implement in the efforts to reach the vision. It is crucial that they feel that they are an integral part of the plan and the planning. Lastly, every action that you and your team take revolves around the vision."

"That's great advice. I'll work on that."

Bill and Jim watched the end of the game as the Packers won again. Jim thanked Bill once more and left for home.

# Chapter 14

The meeting on Tuesday went well, and Craig was very quiet. Jim shared with the team some more details on the reorganization that he had learned, and he also shared with the entire team the definition of vision and how the team was going to go about developing the strategy and the tactics for meeting their vision. As Bill had predicted, Jim's discussions with Mike, as short as they had been, were beginning to lead toward the company's assignment of top-down goals.

It was three o'clock, and Jim was just drained. It had been an exhilarating week, and it had been a challenging week. Then, Alicia appeared at his door.

"Come in," Jim said.

Alicia did, and, as she entered, she shut the door behind her.

Alicia began, "I am very upset about some of the remarks that you have made about me. They were uncalled-for and wrong."

Jim was taken aback. "I have no idea what you are talking about, Alicia."

"You made some remarks to Derek about me being

difficult to work with, being emotional, and being a poor performer. I really don't appreciate that."

Jim was about to deny it when he remembered his discussion with Derek. He was so taken aback that he hesitated.

## Mistake #17: Sharing confidential information or inappropriate remarks about your employees with others.

"That is a really sexist thing to say, and I ought to contact HR," continued Alicia.

"I am sorry, Alicia. You are absolutely correct, and it was certainly the wrong thing to say. I can only tell you that I was overwhelmed with the changes, I misspoke, I apologize, and it will never happen again."

Alicia had been ready for a fight, but Jim's honesty, admission, and apology neutralized her aggressiveness. While she was still angry, there was little more to say.

"I am still upset and don't appreciate your remarks. But, thank you for apologizing," said Alicia. "I have not always been a great performer, but I am determined to do better in the future, and I would appreciate your support in my efforts."

"You will have my support, and I appreciate your willingness to have this honest conversation with me," stated Jim.

"Have a good weekend," Alicia said as she got up and walked out of Jim's office.

At this point, all Jim could do was sit quietly. What a mistake! And why would his good friend Derek share that information when Jim assumed that it was just between the two of them? *That is a lesson learned,* he thought to himself.

Jim was more than ready for the day and the week to end when he heard another knock on his door.

"Come in," he said. It was Craig.

"Hi, Jim, how's it going?"

"Fine," said Jim. "What can I do for you?"

"Jim, I have been thinking about our conversation a couple of weeks ago, and I'm not sure that you and I will ever be able to build a working relationship. I know that my results have not been very good over the past couple of years, but I still believe that I am a top performer and contributor. It is clear to me that the company does not value my experience, so here is my letter of resignation."

"I am surprised," replied Jim.

"Well, I've been looking for a while, and have found this is a great opportunity for me. I am giving you two weeks' notice."

Jim inquired, "So, you are going with a competitor?"

"Yes."

"Then I would like you to clean out your office right now; we will pay you for the two weeks that you have left, but I need for this to be your last day."

"Fine, that is what I expected. I've already packed my stuff, so I'll be leaving within the next ten minutes or so. Best of luck, Jim."

"The best of luck to you also, Craig."

# Chapter 15

Jim and Sarah found a table and ordered dinner. Jim was about to order something with a lot of alcohol in it, but he remembered that Sarah could not have a drink, so he rethought his decision.

"I'll have iced tea," he said.

"Honey, this has been another heck of a couple of weeks," he began.

He then explained some of the positive things that happened however; he spent most of the time on Craig's leaving and his mess-up with Alicia and Derek. Sarah asked a few questions.

"I can't believe that Derek broke our confidence. I think I will say something to him on Monday," Jim finally said.

"Why would you do that?"

"He broke our confidence; I need to say something. I thought he and I were friends."

Sarah astutely observed, "He is your friend, but he is also your subordinate. Your relationship has changed dramatically, and you did not realize that. I think you should be the one to learn the lesson—not Derek."

The truth was difficult to hear, but that was what he

loved about Sarah—she was candid and told it like it was. Jim realized that he needed to be more like that at work.

"You're right. It was a mistake on my part. I just should never have made that mistake, and now Craig is leaving. I just feel that I am making mistake after mistake. I just hate it."

They spent most of the evening talking about Jim's frustration with the mistakes that he had made and his inability to give himself a break.

Sarah suggested that he talk with Bill about this.

## Mistake #18: Failing to understand that you will make mistakes.

## Chapter 16

During his Sunday meeting with Bill, Jim raised the issue of the mistakes he had made. Bill asked whether Jim had informed Mike and Lydia of his conversation with Alicia. He had not.

# Chapter 17

On Monday, Jim made two phone calls. His first call was to Mike to explain that he had made a mistake in sharing his comments and thoughts with Derek. Mike, as usual was distracted, and he told Jim not to worry about it. Mike also asked Jim to call Linda, his assistant, to schedule some time for them to meet. This would allow them to catch up on what was happening. Jim also informed Mike that Craig had resigned; Mike seemed uninterested and transferred Jim to Linda to schedule the meeting.

Linda looked at Mike's calendar and reminded Jim that they had already scheduled monthly meetings. She felt that it would be okay to maintain that schedule.

Jim then called Lydia and shared with her the details of his conversation with Alicia and the underlying cause of that conversation. He was very honest in his evaluation of himself and the fact that he should not have shared any personal or personnel information with Derek or anyone. He also acknowledged that he was very disappointed in Derek's inability to keep information confidential and his willingness to jeopardize their relationship.

## Mistake #19: Not informing the appropriate people when you do make a mistake.

Lydia listened intently and then responded. "Jim," she said, "a couple of things here. There will be many times when you make mistakes; you are human, and we cannot avoid making the mistakes."

"That's what my wife kept telling me all weekend. I just hate making mistakes."

"I am sure you do; we all hate it. But, we are human and can't avoid them," she reminded him. "The issue is how you handle them and what you learn from making those mistakes."

Jim listened carefully, trying to convince himself that she was right.

"In addition," Lydia continued, "You are new in your position; be a bit kind to yourself."

Lydia put on her coaching hat. "Let me follow up on my last comment. Do you believe that you handled the Craig and Alicia issues properly?"

"Well," replied Jim, "I did not do well in the meeting when I lost my temper, which was a real mistake. But, I believe that addressing Craig's behavior immediately and leaving no room for doubt was the right thing to do."

"Even if it resulted in his resigning?"

Jim hesitated. "Uh, yes, I think so."

"I agree 100 percent with you, and I believe that your discussion with him was absolutely the right thing to do. As you had heard, he had been getting away with this for years without being confronted. You did what no other supervisor would do. As a result, you lost a poor performer who had behavior problems. As my kids are learning in school, when you subtract a negative, you get a positive!"

Jim was relieved.

"What about your handling of Alicia?"

"I should never have said anything to Derek."

"I understand that, but I am interested in how you feel that you handled your conversation with her."

Jim felt stronger about this. "I did not feel that I could do anything but tell her the truth and be honest with her. It happened, I made a mistake; I trusted a friend, and I failed to understand that my relationship with him and others had changed. So, I felt that telling the truth and apologizing was the right thing to do. What do you think?"

## Mistake #20: Thinking that integrity is a flexible concept.

Lydia responded, "I believe that you did exactly what you should have done. You were honest, and, while Alicia might not like the fact that you made those comments, she can respect your honesty and high level of integrity in owning up to your mistakes and apologizing. It was the right thing to do, and you should be proud of yourself for making that decision."

# Chapter 18

It was Friday and Jim had made it through another week. It had been a rather uneventful week, for which Jim was grateful. During Tuesday's meeting, Jim asked for the team members' help in developing the strategy and tactics for reaching the vision that he was developing for the team. Jim explained that the vision is at the "left" of the spectrum, while goals are on the "right," and strategy and tactics is in the middle. He also said that, once he had developed the vision, he would be asking for their input in wording it so that it was clear. In the meeting, Jim was asked if he was going to replace Craig; Jim stated that he had not made a decision about that but that all of Craig's accounts had been divided among others, so he felt good about the attention that the clients were receiving. Jim sensed that the team was beginning to come together and that everyone appreciated his openness and honesty, and his efforts to get them involved in some of the decision making. This had not been the case with Gary and Walt.

He was beginning to plan the weekend and how much work he was going to take home. Bill would be out of town this weekend, attending a Wisconsin home game and then

*Management Mistakes*

driving to Minneapolis to watch his Packers battle the Vikings, so Jim had some free time on Sunday.

There was a knock on the door, and Jim looked up to see Alicia at the door.

"Come in," Jim said.

Alicia came in and sat down.

After a bit of small talk, Alicia said, "Jim, the reason I am here is to submit my resignation, effective in two weeks."

For the second time, Jim was taken aback.

Alicia continued, "After our discussion a few weeks ago, I began to think about my life, my career, and your comments. And, while I still do not appreciate your comments to a coworker, they did help me begin to put things in perspective. I realized that I was not happy living here; I do not like my job or the industry, and the fact that I don't have a lot of friends here makes life very difficult. You may or may not know that I come from a family of six kids, and I am the youngest. I was raised on a large farm in Oklahoma, and I just love that flat land. After our discussion and some thinking, I called my dad and talked with him. He is getting up there in age and has for years tried to get one of the kids to take over running the farm. My siblings are all on either the east or west coasts, well into their lives, and they have no interest. So, I told him that if he was still interested, I would love to come back home and run the farm. He and Mom are ecstatic, I am excited, and my brothers and sisters are thankful that they don't have to and that I'll be there to help Mom and Dad as they age. My friends are welcoming me back with open arms."

"I am stunned," replied Jim. "I was hoping that you would not resign, and I am embarrassed that my inappropriate comments precipitated this."

Alicia interrupted, "You need not be embarrassed. I wish that you had not made those remarks to Derek, but, in reality, those remarks moved me to think about my future and address my unhappiness. Inertia would have kept me doing what I did not want to do in a place I did not want to be. So, in reality, you helped me make the move, and I am thankful for that."

Jim and Alicia talked a few more minutes, and she agreed to hold off telling anyone until the Tuesday meeting. She and Jim agreed to meet once more to talk about assigning her clients to her colleagues based on the right fit.

*Create a vision, hire new people, get ready for the Tuesday meeting, prepare for Mike's meeting, think about structure—time to panic,* Jim thought to himself!

# Chapter 19

The weekend was much too short for Jim, but here it was, Monday morning. He had done quite a bit of work on the vision statement, and it seemed ready to present. He had also prepared for his meeting with Mike, although he figured that Mike would do most of the talking. As he was getting started, Julie walked in.

"Morning, Julie."

"It's Monday," Julie said. "I just received a message from Ken, and he said to tell you that he would have a preliminary report ready for you Thursday evening, and he is free on Friday, so if you would like to go over the report on Friday, he would be available."

"That's great; would you schedule something on Friday? Also, would you see if you can find some time today for me to talk with Lydia? Alicia submitted her resignation on Friday."

"I'm not surprised," said Julie. "It was clear to me that she hated her job and just need a push to leave."

"I don't know what I am going to do; I don't like getting two resignations in a row, we need to hire some people," said Jim, with worry in his voice.

"Jim, we are better off without Alicia. I liked her a lot, but she was not happy and just did not care about being successful or making the team successful."

## Mistake #21: Assuming that everyone is engaged in the success of the team.

"I know that you are overwhelmed and this feels like one more thing, but our team will be better off without her and some of the others who don't care."

"There are others?"

"Yes, but that is another conversation."

"I think I'll just jump out the window right now," Jim said resignedly.

"Go ahead," Julie laughed. "You are on the first floor!"

# Chapter 20

The Tuesday meeting began with Jim shaking each attendee's hand as a gesture of appreciation and thanking each one for taking time from his or her busy schedule to attend the meeting. While some thought this a bit hokey, the purpose and message were beginning to sink in—show and express appreciation to your colleagues. Jim began the meeting by announcing that Alicia had submitted her resignation. He asked her to share with the group what her plans were. Everyone was surprised, but no one was shocked. He then mentioned that he would be meeting with Mike on Thursday and with internal auditing on Friday. He added that he would share with them whatever information he could.

Jim then shared his draft of the vision. He handed out a copy to each person and read it aloud: *"To be the top-performing team in our company, as measured primarily by profitability and customer satisfaction scores."*

Jim continued, "I would like to ask each of you to take a look at this vision, have some discussion among yourselves, and offer changes, additions, or deletions. Annette, I know that you have the reputation for being an eloquent and succinct writer, so I would like to ask you to coordinate everyone's ideas. Would that be okay?"

"Sure," replied Annette.

Jim continued, "If everyone can come to agreement on our vision, I would like to ask you to begin working on developing our strategies, which I define as high-level directions; and our tactics, which are very specific actions that we as a group will take in order to reach the goals that the company has set for us and that will also help us reach our vision. Keep in mind that this is a dynamic document, so we'll review it regularly and make strategic and tactic changes as appropriate."

Everyone agreed to the assignment, and they also set a deadline of two weeks for Annette to present a draft of their work.

Jim left the meeting feeling good about the interaction, the team's willingness to participate, and what he saw as movement toward being a cohesive team. Now to prepare for Mike's meeting.

# Chapter 21

"Another Friday," thought Jim. He wasn't sure that Fridays were so great anymore! As he waited for Ken, Jonathan appeared at his door.

"Jim, may I talk with you?" asked Jonathan.

*Not again*, thought Jim. *If another person resigns, I'm quitting!*

"Sure, come in," Jim said.

Jonathan was in his mid-twenties and was the top performer of both teams. He was driven to be successful, did not participate in any gossiping in the office, and worked hard every day. He had been in his job for three years and had quickly moved to the top in performance.

"I wanted you to know that I have been accepted into law school."

"That is great," replied Jim.

"Yes, I've wanted to do this for a while, and this seems like a perfect time for me. But, it is night school so it will take me at least three years to complete, and it is a lot of work. So, I wanted to make sure that you knew what I was doing but also make sure that you knew I wanted to remain with the company and working for you in this position."

"That's great also."

"What I would like to discuss, and maybe we need to talk about this at a later time when you have had time to think about it, is some flexibility in my schedule. I have to be at school four nights a week at 5:30, I have major exams every six weeks, and there is a lot of reading. I want and need this job, I want to be successful in school, but I am not sure that I can do both without some flexibility."

Jim thought for a minute. "Do you know exactly what type of flexibility you want?" he asked.

"No," said Jonathan. "Since I have not even been to class, I have no idea."

"Well, let's postpone our discussion until we both have had a chance to think more about it. I am sure that you'll have an opportunity to talk with some second-year students about what you'll need, and I'll have a chance to think about your request.

"Is that okay?" asked Jim.

"Perfect," said Jonathan. "I'll schedule a meeting within a week or so, through Julie."

"Thanks."

Jim was left to his thoughts—but not for long.

Ken arrived for their meeting. His group had completed a complete internal audit for Jim, and, while the formal report would not be available until the next week, Ken wanted to share with Jim the results and some recommendations.

The audit was very thorough, dealing with expense control, security, physical assets, files, and other aspects of the business. Most of the issues they had uncovered were minor, and Ken offered advice as to how Jim might tighten up the controls without making them so tight as to create resentment. However, some major issues had been found when it came to expenses and the lack of controls under Gary's and Walt's management. In fact, Ken's group had uncovered a multitude of abuses and possible abuses that had occurred. Jim was amazed that senior managers had participated in or, at the very least, been so unconcerned with these abuses. But, as Ken pointed out, that was in the past, and there was nothing anyone could do about it. He provided Jim with some very specific steps, reviewed the company policies with him, and shared some of the best practices being used throughout the company. Jim was very pleased with the results and agreed to put them into place immediately.

# Chapter 22

At their next meeting, Bill and Jim talked a bit about Bill's trip and the fact that the Packers were still undefeated. Since the team was not playing today, they had more time together.

"Tell me what has happened since we last talked," Bill requested of Jim.

Jim reviewed the audit report at a high level and explained the recommendations offered by Ken and his group. Bill congratulated Jim on this approach and his attitude toward internal auditing.

Jim then told Bill that he had created a vision and asked the team to suggest any changes. He also stated that he had asked the team, as a group, to begin developing strategies and tactics for reaching their vision. Jim then shared with Bill his personnel changes. He noted Alicia's leaving and Julie's comments about her lack of commitment.

Bill was able to give Jim some insight on employee commitment. Specifically, he talked about engagement and what the term implies.

"Jim, I think that it would be very worthwhile for you to read the material and research that the Gallup Organization has done on engaged employees. It is eye-opening when you realize that somewhere around 30 percent or so of a company's employees are engaged; the rest are either disengaged or actively disengaged. I suggest that you go to their website and join; this will give you access to their many articles and also to their most recent research."

Jim wrote down the information as he told Bill about Jonathan and his request.

Bill listened intently and then noted that "one of the mistakes that new managers make is trying to treat everyone the same. In fact, not everyone is the same. Some are top performers and some are not.

"In Jack and Suzy Welch's book, *Winning*, they mention the fact that top performers earn chits and others don't. That's a term my generation uses. What they mean is that top performers earn the right to certain benefits, while others do not."

## Mistake #22: Treating top performers like everyone else.

"So my advice would be to think about this seriously and try to determine how you might accommodate his needs and wishes while meeting your goals as well. It sounds like he is someone who you want to keep for the three years he is in law school—and someone who might be valuable to the company in the long term."

Jim agreed and began to gather his belongings.

"You have not said anything about your meeting with Mike, Jim. Did you have it?"

Jim hesitated. "Yes, I did. But, I am telling you, it was as anticlimactic as it could have been. He asked almost no questions, seemed uninterested, continually checked his e-mail, and spent most of the time telling me how difficult his new assignment was. I didn't know if his lack of interest showed faith in me or if he just didn't care. Either way, it was disconcerting and basically a waste of time."

"Interesting," said Bill.

# Chapter 23

Jim was at his desk when the phone rang. Yesterday's meeting with his team had been a good meeting. They had really become involved in developing the strategies and tactics related to the now-agreed-upon vision. Jim was pleased at the way his team members had assumed responsibility for this task. They had been working together to establish strategies and tactics, and Jim had been guiding them. He reminded them often that their strategies and tactics needed to reflect the vision upon which they had all agreed, and that the tactics needed to be measurable and be based on data. The team had decided to do quite a bit of reading on the subject of strategies, tactics, and goals and had come to realize that strategies and tactics were interrelated with execution. They had come to realize that strategies that were poorly executed were not good strategies and that poor strategies never succeed.

**Mistake #23: Not understanding the relationship between strategy, tactics, and execution.**

Jim had taken some time to read about planning and execution, and he had learned quite a great deal from reading Larry Bossidy's book *Execution, The Discipline of Getting Things Done,* which he used as a basis for educating his team on writing a plan. This would help his team draw up the team plan, but Jim also felt that it would help when he asked each of them to develop an individual plan that would guide their actions for the next months. Jim had shared with the team the fact that he had learned that most businesses' plans are drawn up at the company and individual levels, a great deal of work is spent in developing these plans, and then they often are placed in a drawer and never seen again.

Part of what Jim had read centered on the critical issues impacting the business and success. Jim had realized that the majority of his team members never read a business magazine, seldom watched an in-depth business program on television, and never had a discussion at work regarding the big picture and what issues were impacting the company and them as individuals. In fact, Jim bet that half of the employees in his company did not understand how the company made money!

## Mistake #24: Not understanding the critical issues affecting performance and not ensuring that your team understands them as well.

He was also certain that they did not know what issues were impacting their industry and could not explain the current economic conditions to their customers.

# Chapter 24

Jim knew he had a great deal of work to do on this topic and process, but nevertheless he was not happy with the lack of actual performance. He felt that it was time for his team to start producing, since that was the way he and his team were evaluated. Meeting goals and winning were foremost in his mind with everything he did. The group needed to get on board if he was to be successful.

### Mistake #25: Thinking that members of the team are concerned about your success.

Jim answered the phone. It was Lydia from HR.

"Jim," she stated, "This is Lydia. Do you have some time to talk with me?"

"Yes, I do," he answered.

Lydia continued, "We have completed the personnel audit that you requested, and I will be sending you the results in the interoffice mail, but I wanted you to know that we found some very serious and disturbing discrepancies.

You were absolutely correct in your assessment of possible issues."

"Give me an overview of what you found, please," Jim requested.

"We looked at both your professional team and your staff personnel. We found no issues within your staff, but we did find some serious issues within your professional team."

"First, the makeup of Gary's old team does not reflect the general makeup of our company in general, and that is of some concern."

"Give me the details."

"Gary's team has one female out of eight professionals, that's about 12 percent. Of the professionals within our company, females make up of about 65 percent of the total. Walt's team is 60 percent female, so we are not concerned about that; the minority profile is also not a concern. The biggest discrepancy is in the salary difference between men and women. Our HR consulting firm ran a statistical analysis using education, experience, time in the industry, time with our company, and annual appraisal rating, and found that, on average, females on the two teams make about $6,500 less per year than males. This is concerning, serious, and clearly could be the grounds for a lawsuit."

"How long has this been going on?" asked Jim.

"It looks like it has been a gradual process for a number of years."

Jim asked, "How do we resolve this?"

"First, just to let you know, we have informed the head of HR, and she has taken this to the HR Committee of the Board, so that they are aware of the issue. Second, we have decided to give the females on the team an increase to bring their salaries up to the same level as their male counterparts. Third, at the end of the year when bonuses are

*Management Mistakes*

awarded, we will be assigning a significant amount to you for distribution to the females on your team to compensate for years of inequity. This amount will be outside the normal bonus amount, and we will give you the numbers for each woman."

"That's great," said Jim.

Lydia continued, "This is very sensitive, Jim. Once you receive the material, we would like for you to meet with each woman individually and confidentially. You will tell them that you reviewed their performance and their salary and felt that their current salary did not reflect their contribution to the company. Thus, you recommended to HR that the company raise the individual's salary, and that was approved. Using the data that I send you, you can use the numbers shown and tell each individual that the new salary will be effective in the next paycheck. Do not mention anything about the review, our conversation, or the end-of-year bonuses. We do not want this to become a companywide issue. In addition, ask each person to keep the information confidential."

"How can something like this happen, Lydia? How can HR not complete these types of reviews? Did anyone else in the company have any idea?"

Lydia hesitated a bit and then said, "We have process in place for analyzing salaries and increases as they relate to various factors. This is completed by an HR analysis firm that we contract; they just did not do their job."

She added, "Also, at the end of the year, when you get ready to recommend raises, you and I will meet and discuss. Once we agree on the numbers, that data will go to your boss and his HR partner for sign-off."

"Did these recommendations go to Mike?"

"Yes," Lydia stated.

"And, how about the recommendations that Gary and Walt made over the years?" asked Jim.

"Mike reviewed the recommendations each year."

There was a quiet pause between Lydia and Jim after she made that statement.

"Okay, send me the material and I will meet with each individually and privately, share the information, and ask each employee to not share the information. I will not say anything about the end-of-year bonuses until I am asked to."

"You will receive the entire package in a couple of days. Thanks, and let me know how it goes."

# Chapter 25

Once again it was Friday, and Jim had scheduled a meeting with Jonathan to discuss his situation—although Jim was never sure what Friday would bring!

Jonathan arrived, and Jim started immediately. He briefly reviewed Jonathan's request and asked him what he had learned from the second-year students. He thanked Jonathan for being such a top producer and then talked specifics. "Jonathan, I appreciate all that you have done to make this team successful and also your desire to become a lawyer. So, here is my proposal. You can come to work when you want and you can leave work each day when you need to; I am fine with that. Also, I know that law school exams are challenging at the very least, so you should feel free to take the week before your exams off, and I will not count that as any type of leave or vacation. In return, I am asking for three things: that you meet the goals assigned to you, that you score at or above the expected level on the customer satisfaction scores that are produced each quarter, and that you receive no customer complaints. How do feel about those conditions?"

"That is great," said Jonathan.

"Well, I really appreciate your past performance, know you want to remain with the company, and believe that the company would benefit from your remaining with us, so I want to do as much as I can to keep you here. We'll review your performance against the three factors that I have mentioned quarterly. As long as you meet the requirements, we'll continue with our agreement."

"Thanks, Jim. I really appreciate your accommodating my school needs."

# Chapter 26

Jim and Bill watched the end of the Packers game and then Jim proceeded to bring Bill up to date. But, Jim really wanted to talk about performance.

"The team has really done a great job of creating a strategic plan and tactics around the vision statement. They actually did not change the statement at all."

"So, you think that they have all bought into the vision?"

"In varying degrees," Jim said. "I am not sure that I can ever get them to be 100 percent in agreement to everything, but they have all been involved and have contributed something."

"That's a real tribute to your leadership."

Jim continued, "The real issue that I am having is performance measurements and how I am going to track and monitor what they are doing in order to move the level of performance higher."

"What are you thinking?" asked Bill.

Jim went through his thinking, including his one-page measurement system, his weekly report from every producer, the documents that he had created, and the weekly pipeline report. He wanted to know exactly what each team member was doing.

Bill thought for a minute and then asked, "If this group was so good at accepting the vision, creating the strategic direction, and creating the tactics associated with meeting the company goals, what makes you think that they will not perform?"

"They have never performed very well. The only reason that they have been in the middle of team performance rankings is that there are three or four really top performers. I've looked at the numbers for the past four years and analyzed them, and when you do that it really stands out that just a few are carrying the entire team. I want to make sure that everyone is carrying his or her own weight."

## Mistake #26: Not using data to manage.

"I want this to be the best team in the company!"

"I understand that," said Bill. "What gives you the idea that they are not committed to the same goal? They took your strategy challenge and, according to you, are doing a great job."

Jim was silent.

"Earlier in our series of meetings, you stated that you were going to meet with each team member individually before going through the personnel files. Have you been through the files?"

Jim admitted that he had not.

"And have you met with each person?"

Again, Jim responded with a no.

"And why not? Don't you think that it is important to understand each member of your team?"

"I just have not had the time," said Jim. "Things have just been so busy."

Bill coached Jim, "I am having a difficult time understanding why you want to implement very detailed management reporting and documentation when you have not had a personal discussion with each employee to try to determine his or her commitment to success. You may well have to create some detailed reporting around activities that are known to create success for those who do not exhibit those qualities, but first you need to determine who is committed, who has the skills, and who executes those skills."

Jim was quiet once again.

## Mistake #27: Micromanaging.

"You were willing to create a flexible program for Jonathan because you knew he was committed and that he was a top performer; why would you not be willing to take that time with everyone? Creating a micromanagement philosophy for everyone will drive your top performers out of your team and possibly out of the company very quickly."

Bill continued, " "My advice is to hold off on implementing any such policy or procedures before you have had a chance to meet with every single employee, take a temperature check on his or her commitment to the vision, and determine how well each executes his or her plan to succeed."

## Chapter 27

Jim sat quietly at home, thinking about Bill's comments. On Monday, he planned to ask Julie to begin scheduling time with each team member. He also began developing an agenda that he would follow in talking with each person.

Monday morning, Jim wasted no time.

"Julie," Jim said, "I would like to meet with every person one-on-one, starting tomorrow. Would you mind scheduling those meetings?"

"How long should each meeting be?"

"I am thinking that we should schedule two hour per person. Also, please make sure that I don't have anything scheduled for a half hour after each meeting, since I don't want to feel rushed. I will be placing my phone on forward to you, and I am going to silence the incoming e-mail notification so that each person will have my undivided attention."

**Mistake #28: Being too busy or distracted to listen intently.**

*Management Mistakes*

Jim began to develop an agenda for himself so that he could be organized.

He was interrupted by the phone ringing. He answered it. The person calling was Christine. He had never met Christine, but he knew of her reputation. She was Mike's boss and had a reputation for being tough with high expectations, extremely fair, and she always exhibited a very high standard of integrity.

"Hi, Jim," said Christine.

"Good morning," replied Jim.

"I am calling for a couple of reasons. The first is to thank you for recognizing the need for a personnel audit as you took a leadership position within our company. I apologize that you had to ask for one, but I am very proud of you for recognizing the need. Certainly the result of the personnel audit was disturbing, but your action allows us to correct a bad situation and to change our company procedures. Second, I appreciate your relationship with our internal auditing department. Ken has shared with me some of your comments and his growing relationship with you, and I appreciate that attitude. In the near future, I am going to ask you to share your philosophy and how you developed it with others in our company. We've got to change the relationships within our company, and I am convinced that you are the person to be our catalyst."

Jim thanked her, and she continued.

"Lastly, Lydia has shared with me your approach to developing a vision and then strategies and tactics that support that strategy as you try to reach your goals. You've done a great job, and I am very proud of the progress that you have made in a relatively short time."

"Thank you again," said Jim.

"You are certainly welcome. Some questions for you: I know that the economic times are difficult, but I would like to know the general health of your clients, what percentage of your loan requests are being approved, what are the reasons for any declines, how long is the time from submission of the application to funding, and, if you and your team could change anything, what would it be?"

Jim paused for a moment. He did not know the answers to the questions and hated to say that he did not know. Making up answers would certainly get him in trouble if his answers were not accurate.

"Christine, I apologize but I don't know the answers to your questions." This was difficult for him to say because it made him feel that he should know the answers and that he was, once again, making a mistake.

Christine answered, "Jim, there will be instances where you do not know the answer to a question. We deal with so much every day that you cannot be expected to know every detail."

## Mistake #29: Believing that you cannot say, "I don't know."

"Of course, saying 'I don't know' to every question isn't acceptable either. As you spend more time managing and leading, you'll get an idea as to what is important and what you should know, versus what is less important and what you can look up. It is okay to say that you don't know; get back to me when you can.

"Thanks again for everything that you have done and are doing, Jim," Christine concluded.

# Chapter 28

Jim spent the rest of the day working on the agenda for the individual employee meetings that would start the next day. Julie had scheduled most of them, so Jim knew that he would be completing all of them within two weeks. His agenda, for his eyes only, when finalized, gave him a roadmap for the meetings:
- Forward phone
- Silence computer
- Explain time (an hour; not set in stone, will take as long as needed)
- Open and candid conversation
- Stated purpose to each individual:
- Get to know person
- Ask for ideas and suggestions
- Help with career
- Understand how he could make work more fun
- Unmentioned purposes:
- Determine strengths and weaknesses
- Try to understand commitment to team
- Estimate engagement with the company

- Determine if the individual practices behaviors and activities proven to improve success

Jim had also read thoroughly the research that Gallup had produced and studied their twelve questions that determine engagement. On his list of things to do was to contact the marketing and HR departments to see if they could research a contract with Gallup to use the questions on a companywide basis—starting with his team.

## Chapter 29

For the next two weeks, Jim spent much of his time talking with each team member and following, as closely as possible, his agenda. It was very informative, and Jim was learning a great deal about his people. The downside of this process was that, during their meetings, Howard submitted his retirement letter; Bonnie announced that her husband, a Marine, had received his transfer orders to North Carolina; and Jean informed Jim that she had accepted a position at another institution. Even with the salary increase that Jim shared with her, she decided to leave and go with a competitor. While Jim was pleased with everything that he was learning, he was also concerned about replacing the five team members who had left or announced they were leaving.

During his time with Bill on Sunday, Jim focused on replacing the team members. Bill asked a lot of questions about duties and performance. Ultimately, Jim stated that he felt that the five could be replaced by three top performers who were engaged.

Jim told Bill that he had discussed the open positions with the recruiting team and told them that, if he was going to meet his goals this year, he needed to replace these individuals as quickly as possible. Bill listened carefully and then asked Jim how long he thought it would take to interview, choose, do background checks, and make offers.

Jim stated, "Two weeks."

"And do you believe that your team is better off with these five leaving?"

"Absolutely," said Jim.

"And do you believe that the three who are replacing the five must be top performers?"

"Yes."

"Do you believe that team members must fit in with the other members, that a team has a character, and that all team members must fit in?"

"Of course I do."

"Then, Jim, if you believe all of these things, why would you expect to fill any position, let alone three positions, in two weeks? There is a phrase, 'easy to hire, hard to fire,' that you need to consider. It is always easy to hire someone, but it is very difficult to get rid of them if they are not the right person."

"But I am concerned about meeting my goals."

## Mistake #30: Not taking the time to hire the right people.

"I understand that," said Bill, "but you need to consider what you just said. If you hire the wrong person or people, someone who does not fit in, who turns out not to be a top performer, or who undermines what you are trying to do, you have then sabotaged your team and all of the accomplishments that you have produced so far. It is better to be down someone than to hire the wrong person."

# Chapter 30

Jim's Tuesday meetings had turned into rigorous sessions with lots of discussion. While they were taking longer than Jim would like, he realized that the passion and engagement that each team member was showing indicated their commitment to the success of the team. Even Julie had mentioned to him that she had never seen anything like this before. At the last meeting, he had been asked about where they stood against the rest of the teams in the company. Jim realized that, while he had developed a dashboard for his own use, he was not sharing the results with his team as often as he should be.

## Mistake #31: Not regularly keeping the team focused on results.

Since that last meeting, Jim had changed his dashboard a bit, added a few items, and made it easier to read. It was a bit difficult to produce each week, since Jim had to retrieve and manipulate much of the data manually. But, Jim was sure that this document had been and would continue to be one of the motivators of his team and one of the things that kept his team focused. He had put together a group of competitive individuals, and competitive individuals need to know how they are doing and where they stand in order to stay focused.

Bill had told Jim a story about one group he managed early in his career. He had tried to understand what motivated each person and had actually asked each that question in one of the one-on-one meetings he had with his employees. The first individual was motivated by money: pay him more, give him a good incentive plan, it did not matter. The second was motivated by standings. She did not care about money but was driven to be number one in anything and everything. Bill had figured this out, so he published rankings at the end of each week to keep her motivated. The third was motivated by recognition. Money was unimportant and even rankings were not that crucial; but a fax, a card, a phone call or some other form of recognition drove this person to perform. Bill laughed when he told this story because, using his personal motivation techniques, he had the three top performers on the entire East Coast on his team.

## Mistake #32: Not understanding what motivates each individual.

# Chapter 31

Jim settled back into his chair. It had been nine months since he had taken over, and, while he was not feeling overly confident about managing, he was feeling good about his accomplishments.

Jim was also learning how to determine what issues needed addressing and which ones would take care of themselves. In many cases, issues arose between two individuals who wanted Jim to referee their argument. Jim had learned to push these issues back to the individuals and expect them to communicate and solve their own problems. This had reduced the number of minor complaints, since his team had learned that they were going to have to act like adults.

## Mistake #33: Sweating the small stuff while missing the important things.

He could not help remembering his two trips to corporate headquarters to explain how he had accomplished so much in such a short time and to explain why his team was performing so well in a questionable economy. *It was interesting*; he thought to himself, *that Mike had not been present at those meetings.*

Jim was proud of his team, and that was really the message that he gave to the people at corporate: get people engaged, give them some authority, and provide feedback on their progress. Jim praised his team and gave them the credit for making such great progress.

Jim had become known for his thank-you notes, his crazy presentations in meetings to people who deserved recognition, and even for sending gifts to the partner or spouse of an employee who had worked hard, thanking that partner for his or her support during a challenging time. It was so easy that he often wondered why others did not do it more often.

## Mistake #34: Not giving your people credit and recognition for every success.

Jim always copied Mike on his notes of thanks and recognition, and he often asked Mike to send an e-mail or to call the individual. This was out of Mike's circle of comfort, but he did it anyway. Jim's actions had become well-known within the company. Jim realized that, with all of the notes, e-mails, and phone calls pertaining to great service his team was becoming known as the best in the company. He did not know if this was true—but he did understand that perception is reality!

## **Chapter 32**

"Jim," Julie interrupted his thoughts. "Christine just called and said to let you know that she was going to be in town this Friday and would like to have some time with you. She said that sometime around two o'clock would be perfect."

Julie continued, "I scheduled her for two o'clock, since you did not have anything after that on your calendar."

"Thanks, Julie," responded Jim. "I wonder what she is doing in town."

# Chapter 33

Friday arrived, and Jim joked to himself that his work life always changed on Fridays, and, with Christine visiting from corporate headquarters, who knew what this Friday would bring.

Christine entered his office.

"Hi, Jim. Is this a good time for you?"

"Of course," said Jim.

"First, let me congratulate you and Sarah on the birth of your twins. I hope that everyone is doing well."

Jim could hardly contain his excitement. "Everyone is doing fine; Sarah is great, and the twins are just amazing."

"Well, I have an eleven-, nine-, and five-year-old, so let me assure you that having kids doesn't change your life very much!"

They both laughed.

"Seriously, on that matter, I hope that you will keep your family in perspective. Most companies talk about balance, but, in reality, your family is the most important thing in your life and kids grow up much too fast."

"Thanks very much," said Jim.

"Let me get to the point," Christine continued. "Everyone

*Management Mistakes*

at the senior management level has appreciated everything that you have done in the past nine or ten months. You have really made a difference. On the recent companywide attitude survey, your team had the highest satisfaction scores—they were the happiest at work and were the most engaged of any team within our company. When added to the fact that your team is the top performing team in the company, your results have been almost miraculous. Of course, we all know that it was not a miracle—it was hard work, focus, and empowering your team."

"I am overwhelmed at the compliments," said Jim.

"Well," Christine said with a smile, "if you are overwhelmed with that, this might really overwhelm you: I am in town today to relieve Mike of his responsibilities. As of now, he is no longer with our company."

Jim was surprised but not shocked, based on Mike's lack of communication, lack of leadership, and inability to improve the performance of his new division.

"We are promoting you to division head, replacing Mike, and asking you to take that position effective as soon as we make the announcement Monday morning. Julie will be going with you, and both of you will be moving into Mike's suite. We will expect you to fill this position but have no expectations as to any timeframe, since we know that you do not hire without a thorough process. You have the support of every senior manager in the company and should feel free to call on any resources available."

# Appendix A

In this appendix, we'll expand on the mistakes that Jim made—or could have made. Appendix provides actual examples.

## 1. Thinking You Can Do It All Yourself and Not Seeking Help

Experienced managers understand that they need help from experts within an organization to create change. A common mistake seen with new managers is their belief that they can do it all by themselves. You need to remember that you only have so much time and you only have so much expertise. It is crucial to call on others within your company who have the expertise to help you create change. Some of those individuals from whom you can seek assistance have great reputations for being experts, being great partners, and helping others move the company in the right direction. Others do not; stay away from them.

If you try to do everything by yourself, you will:
- Not accomplish what you want to accomplish
- Develop a reputation for mediocrity
- Burn out

Determine when and with what you need help, find out whom in your company can be trusted and who has a reputation for action, determine the exact help needed—then ask for it.

Finally, manage the process.

## 2. Believing That You Can Change Everything Quickly

Many new managers believe that they understand what the issues are, and many have a desire to create change quickly. That belief is certainly admirable, but it is a false belief and one that can lead to failure. "You can't boil the ocean" is an often-used statement, and this is a good example.

Instead of trying to correct everything at once, categorize the issues and tackle them one at a time. Start with those issues that are irritating and that distract your team. Deal with these quickly, once and for all.

Then tackle those issues that have a negative impact on the performance of your team. Your job is to get the team performing at a high level; develop your strategy, execute your tactics, and focus on those difficult issues that impact performance.

It is easy for you to be distracted by minor issues that really do not have any significant impact on your team's performance. In many cases, these issues will take care of themselves over time.

### 3. Not Preparing For Meetings When You Are In Charge

"Being prepared" means controlling the meetings, reaching outcomes, and dealing with distractions among the attendees.

Critical elements of "being prepared" include:

- Starting on time and ending on time; being respectful of everyone's time is important
- Understanding what you want the outcome of the meeting to be in advance
- Understanding and managing the dynamics that exist among the attendees
- Creating an agenda, circulating it before the meeting, asking for additional items, and sticking to the agenda
- Taking notes; do not delegate this task; taking notes is a sign of being in charge
- Recording decisions, assignments, and to-do items
- Reiterating your vision during the meetings
- Controlling outbursts

### 4. Forgetting That Family Is Everything and Should Always Come First

I once worked with a senior vice president who was one of the brightest individuals with whom I have worked. A graduate of an Ivy League school, he worked seven days a week, traveled regularly, and was a top performer. He seldom made it home before 8 p.m., usually left home before 6 a.m., always worked on Saturday and Sunday, and thus seldom saw the great adventure of his kids growing up. He was a great performer at work, and many envied his stature within the company.

The sad ending of this story is that, when the company got into trouble, he was called to headquarters and informed that he no longer had a position. Upon returning home, he found that his wife and children had left. His spouse had had enough, and the family never reconciled.

## 5. Reviewing Personnel Files Before You Have a Chance to Draw Your Own Conclusions

As a teacher and administrator, I told parents and teachers alike that I had never met a kid who came to school and wanted to fail. After forty-two years of managing, I feel the same way about employees. I have never met an employee who wanted to fail. Personnel files never tell why someone fails; they only show that someone failed (or succeeded).

These files never reveal the supervisor, his or her approach, or the situations in which the employee succeeded or failed.

As you take over a new team, watch, listen, talk to, evaluate, and make up your own mind about each individual. Tom Peters coined the term "management by walking around." Be visible, walk around! Your job is to understand each employee and motivate that employee to perform at a level that exceeds expectations; understand and evaluate—then take a look at the files.

## 6. Not Understanding That Once You Are Promoted, Relationships Change

No matter who you are, a promotion changes your relationship with everyone. You have power that you did not have, and that changes everything. While some of your former colleagues, now subordinates, may choose to believe that nothing has changed, it is crucial for you to recognize that *everything* has changed. You can no longer opine with your colleagues about the company, its leaders, and the issues within the company.

In addition, you are now privy to information that others in the company are not and should not know. This requires you to keep that information confidential.

This does not mean that you cannot remains friends with your former colleagues, but it does mean that you cannot share certain information with them, you cannot treat them as equals, and you must always remain cognizant of the role of management.

There are many stories about new managers who, after a few drinks with their former peers, shared too much information or made inappropriate comments. Control yourself and control your alcohol intake (more about this later).

## 7. Not Maintaining Control

The previous mistake dealt with self-control; this issue is about control of your employees. There is a fine line between allowing people to express their opinions, even whine a bit, and being out of control. You must learn the difference.

As you learn the difference, you must always remember that any comments that are discriminatory, off-color, or inappropriate must be dealt with immediately and firmly. As the senior person in the meeting or department, you can be held personally liable in a lawsuit—not to mention your professional responsibility and potential damage to your reputation.

Accept no compromise in maintaining control.

Accept no compromise in managing and reporting out-of-control behavior.

8. **Not Choosing a Good Assistant and/or Not Treating That Assistant as an Important Partner**

Too many new managers and many experienced managers treat their assistants as just another employee. This is a huge mistake. It not only wastes an enormous opportunity for a partnership, it can lead to not having that person's support when needed.

In the middle of my career, I had the fortunate opportunity to work with an assistant who was talented and experienced. Our relationship became one of respect and partnership. Many times during our eight years of working together, she cautioned me on actions I was going to take, phone calls I was about to make, and memos I was about to write. As I am someone who had a tendency toward "ready, fire, aim," she was an invaluable resource for me.

She was also my advocate, and numerous times she explained in language that others could understand what I was trying to do—clearing up confusion and providing support for me.

This individual will be the closest to you of anyone who reports to you; therefore, you must treat this person with respect, ask for advice, and develop a candid and honest relationship. If, after spending time with this individual, you feel that the trust and open relationship cannot develop, make a change. Do not continue a relationship that is not built on trust and openness.

## 9. Ready, Fire, Aim

For Type A managers, those "get it done, make a decision" people, taking time to think through a situation can be a painful exercise. Add to this situation the stress of not having enough time, and making quick decisions becomes paramount for some managers. Do not let this become your style of managing and making decisions.

Failure to understand the situation, the facts surrounding the situation, and the impact of your decisions always leads to bad decisions. Impatient decisions never lead to good conclusions! It can also lead to reputational risk and limit your career advancement.

There will be few situations during your career that require an immediate decision. Understand the issues, get the facts, remember that every story has multiple sides, reduce your personal feelings, and then make your decisions, keeping in mind the vision, strategies, and values of the company.

## 10. **Not Seeing Internal Auditing as an Ally**

Auditors are a different breed, and you need to understand that. Linear thinkers, black-and-white, and concrete sequential are some of the adjectives that might be used to describe them. Adversaries and enemies are not terms that should be used!

When you begin your management career, decide immediately that this group will be your friend and ally, and know that they are going to be an asset during your entire career. Here's the reason: they have no vested interest in anything except reducing losses, adhering to established rules, developing controls, improving processes, and other such issues. None of these should threaten you as a manager. In fact, the chances of you being fired for lax controls or losses are much higher than the chance of being fired for poor performance.

On the plus side, this group can protect you from mistakes made by the former manager, of which you had no knowledge. Even if you are not blamed, you will spend precious time explaining the situation, what happened, and why you should not be blamed. This group is your friend; use them to your advantage.

## 11. Not Setting a Baseline for Everything

While this mistake can be related to the failure to see auditors as a friend, that is only part of the picture. Developing and establishing a baseline for everything is simply a way to know where you are when you start the race. It is also a way to protect yourself.

Failure to develop the baseline leaves you vulnerable to either being held responsible for the mistakes of your predecessor, or, at the very least, spending valuable time and energy explaining why something happened on your watch.

A new manager taking over a department that contracted some of its services chose to develop a baseline for everything. The manager included the manner in which audits of the vendor were conducted. By asking questions of the audit department that were not normally asked, the new manager uncovered some serious discrepancies and brought those to the attention of senior management. This resulted in a change to the audit procedures and the recovery of $6 million from the third-party vendor.

## 12. Not Addressing Inappropriate Behavior Immediately

Managing people remotely is always difficult. It is difficult to determine how people are being treated by their managers. Years ago, I began to hear rumors about the behavior of one of my direct reports, whom I managed remotely and had inherited from another senior manager. Upon hearing the rumors, I made an unannounced visit—only to learn that he was having a two o'clock lunch at a local bar. After calling him on his cell phone (what a surprise for him), we met back at his office. I confronted him on the rumors that I had been hearing; he denied everything vehemently. To conduct an investigation, I suspended him with pay until I could interview all of his employees. Within four hours of my suspension, he called and resigned.

Any inappropriate behavior or comments must be dealt with immediately and clearly. You cannot let any situation that is not professional go by without addressing it.

This includes subtle remarks and actions; you need to be constantly aware of any inappropriate remarks regarding sex, race, or sexual preference. This includes off-color jokes or jokes that refer to any of the above. In addition, you cannot participate by telling such jokes—or even laughing at those jokes.

Inappropriate behavior includes actions in meetings and comments about the company.

Much of this can be avoided if, in the early part of your tenure, you give your "inappropriate behavior" speech which specifies what you will not tolerate.

## 13. Not Apologizing When You Make a Mistake

Why is it that, when people attain powerful positions, they forget to apologize when they make a mistake? A trait learned at the earliest age, expected by most parents, and a set of words that are so well-received—yet many managers feel that it is beneath them to say "I'm sorry."

As a senior vice president, I was introduced to a corporate trainer and asked to share my opinion about a particular aspect of training that was impacting my division. Having been a teacher for fourteen years, I shared my concerns and dissatisfaction in a professional manner. In fact, I was informed by an individual who was present that my remarks were professional and right on target.

Later, I discovered that the trainer had been very upset and had taken my remarks very personally. I called her, apologized that my remarks had upset her, and told her that upsetting her was never my intention. She was gracious and thanked me for my apology.

The fact that I had apologized went like wildfire through the entire training department because, in the company at that time, no senior vice president had ever apologized for anything—including being wrong. The attitude was that they were just too important to apologize.

From that day on, the training department was more than willing to help me with anything I needed and make changes based on my suggestions. People were so accustomed to the arrogance of the management team that a simple apology worked magic (and made me feel better also). Is there any question as to why this company ultimately failed?

## 14. Not Properly Documenting Conversations About Performance or Behavior

Documentation of conversations is crucial for two reasons. First, it gives you a record of the conversation. If you do not keep a record of the conversation, the content becomes a matter of opinion. This is never a good situation.

Second, the documentation becomes a source of facts, should there be any type of dispute, legal or not.

Take notes during the meeting, review and rewrite those notes in summary form, give a copy to the other party, ask that party to make any changes—subject to your agreement—and sign that he or she received a copy. Place a signed copy in the individual's file.

### 15. Talking More Than You Listen

For some reason, when some people become managers, they feel that they need to do all of the talking. I once attended a meeting with the new president of our company, who, when introduced, stated that he had been given twenty minutes on the agenda but that "he would take as long as he wanted because he was in charge!" He then proceeded to talk for over an hour.

What makes managers go from individual performers who would like to be heard and have input to managers who do all of the talking? Maybe its knowledge, maybe it is the power or maybe it is something else. Whatever you do, talk less than you listen. First of all, you'll learn a great deal. Your employees understand what is happening, what the issues are—and you can learn what going on if you listen. Second, it keeps your employees engaged. Your employees want to feel as if they are valued (read *Drive,* by Daniel Pink, to learn more about what motivates people). Third, listening attentively assures the rest of your team that you are not arrogant and that you actually value their input.

Your success is measured by the performance of your team—not how much you can talk or how much you know.

## 16. Not Creating and Articulating a Vision of the Future

While most of us do not have a vision when we are young, we develop a vision as we age. We may not put it on paper (or computer), but we still have in our minds a vision of what we would like to accomplish. Most life coaches suggest that we place our vision on paper in order to solidify it.

This same approach applies to developing a vision for your team. They need to know the road that they will travel and understand what it will look like when they arrive.

If you do not know how to write a vision, buy a book that explains what visions are, what they are intended to do, and how to write one. Once you have developed a vision, reiterate it often and clearly, and ensure that every decision guides you and your team toward that vision.

A Fortune 500 company was in the habit of creating a new vision every six months or so; needless to say, the employees had no idea what the vision of the company really was or if they were going in the right direction!

## 17. Sharing Confidential Information About Your Employees with Others

There are three factors that you need to understand when it comes to confidential information: alcohol, friendships, and that information is power.

You cannot, as a manager, share any confidential information with others. Most of the time this rule involves personal or performance information about someone on your team, but it also applies to company information.

This is one of the most common issues for new managers. There are many opportunities to share confidential information. Information is power, and it is fun to share information that others don't have; it makes people feel really important. Don't fall victim to that common temptation.

Friendships are built at work; it is one of Gallup's twelve questions. We all know that these friendships are important. Unfortunately, for new managers who are now isolated from others, these friendships represent one of the sinkholes that can derail careers. It is easy for a new manager to be drawn into situations where he or she shares just a tidbit of information about another employee (or the company) with a friend. Don't fall victim to this situation.

The new CEO announces a promotion and then tells an employee who reports to the newly-promoted individual that he is not sure she is "up to the job." An executive vice president shares with another employee that someone is going to get fired for poor performance. What do these two situations have in common? Alcohol! In both cases, the manager was drinking with employees and failed to understand the impact of alcohol on the conversation. Your career, reputation, and respect are not worth a few drinks. Do not fall victim to this situation.

## 18. Failing to Understand That You Will Make Mistakes

Humans make mistakes. Let me repeat, humans make mistakes! As a human, you will make a lot of mistakes during your management career. So, here's the advice:

- Learn from your mistakes. There is no reason why you should make the same mistake twice.
- Correct mistakes quickly; have a plan and execute that plan.
- Apologize if necessary; it's not that hard, and an apology goes a long way.
- Never cover up a mistake. First, you can't; second, it never pays. Repeat after me: Pete Rose, Richard Nixon, and Martha Stewart.
- Make sure the right people know that you made a mistake and that you have a plan of action for correcting it. Execute that plan!

## 19. Not Informing the Appropriate People When You Have Made a Mistake

Mistakes are bound to happen, whether they are your mistakes or mistakes made by someone who works for you. If the mistakes are made by someone who works for you, you need to know about those mistakes as soon as possible. First, the sooner you learn about the mistake, the faster you can develop a strategy for correcting it. Second, the last thing you want is for your boss to hear about the mistake before you do. There is no good outcome from your boss learning before you do.

Therefore, you must create an atmosphere where your employees tell you about mistakes truthfully and quickly. Not only minor mistakes, but mistakes that fall under the illegal, immoral, reputation, or other such categories of mistakes. You must create an open atmosphere, and you must educate your employees about sharing the mistakes with you immediately.

This same philosophy applies to you and your relationship with your boss. You must inform your boss regarding mistakes. When you do share the information, it must be clear, accurate, and include a description of how you plan to fix it.

Finally, remember that the cover-up is always worse than the mistake. If you don't believe that then, once again, think about Richard Nixon, Martha Stewart, Pete Rose, and, add Penn State.

## 20. Thinking That Integrity Is a Flexible Concept

It does not matter what your business is or where you stand in the corporate hierarchy—your honor, trust, and integrity are ultimately all you have as an individual and as a company. These values apply to all aspects of your life and your business, no matter how large or small. When I was working for a publicly traded company, the chairman was consistently stating publicly that he was through with acquisitions and was going to start focusing on improving core performance. He would then turn around and purchase another company. Wall Street never trusted his word, and the company's performance on Wall Street suffered.

An individual in another company is told sensitive information, with the understanding that it is to be kept secret. The individual shares that information with someone else, who shares it, and so on—until someone three levels up has a conversation with the first individual.

Integrity is not a gray area, and it is not a "flexible concept" to be adapted to the situation at hand. Many careers have been ruined because individuals did not understand that rule.

As a new manager, I was responsible for approving the loan requests of individuals who worked for me. Upon reviewing an application, I chose not to approve it; the person who had submitted it then asked my boss to look at it. He and I discussed it, and he advised me to approve it. When I asked him to sign on the approval with me, he would not. Asked why, he stated that he did not trust the individual to pay it back. I realized that he was letting me step out on that plank without any support. Needless to say, I never trusted him again.

On the other hand, in the same organization, when I was hired, the hiring manager stated that, in six months,

*Management Mistakes*

I would receive a substantial raise. The six months came, and I was a bit hesitant to question him about it; but the first paycheck after my six months showed a significant raise—exactly as he had promised!

## 21. Assuming That Everyone Is Engaged in the Success of the Team

Years ago, I coached both wrestling and baseball at the high school level. The first comments from parents as kids got off the bus from an away game have stuck with me throughout my business career. Baseball is a team sport; there are no individual winners. So, when the bus arrived and kids started pouring out, the first question asked by the parents was, "Did the team win?" Wrestling, on the other hand, is an individual sport where individuals win or lose and the number of winners and losers determines whether the team wins or loses. When this bus arrived and the kids got off the bus, the first question asked by parents was, "Did *you* win?"

Your team members are wrestlers—they are judged, evaluated, paid, and incentivized on their individual performance. Thus they are individual performers. While they may like to be part of a winning team and rejoice over the accolades associated with being part of a winning team, they are focused on themselves first. They will not hit a sacrifice fly for the team!

You need to remember that fact. Your job is to try to coordinate their individual performance so that it produces team results.

## 22. Treating Top Performers Like Everyone Else

Top performers are different from the others on your team; they are top performers! In Jack Welch's books *From the Gut* and *Winning,* he is very clear that top performers should be treated differently because they earn it. Good kids get privileges, great athletes receive big contracts, and top performers earn "chits."

The contract is that an employee who a top performer is treated differently. If an average employee complains, that is the contract you then hand him or her. Become a top performer, earn privileges!

While managing a wealth management division for a large bank, I was approached by a young man who was about to begin his last year of MBA school and start his first year of law school at the same time. I had promoted him a year or so earlier, and he had become one of my top performers. In fact, he was the second-highest performer against goals in a six-state region. He asked for some leeway in his hours so that he could attend class each night.

After some discussion, I made a deal with him. He could come in anytime he wanted, leave anytime he wanted, and take the week before each exam off without recording it as vacation—as long as he met his goals, received no customer complaints, and scored in the top 10 percent on the quarterly customer surveys conducted by Gallup for our organization. He accepted the terms of our agreement.

Throughout the next year, he came and went as he chose, took the week off before exams to study, and remained the second-highest performer in the region, with some of the highest customer survey scores and not one customer complaint.

When some of his colleagues made comments about

his flexible schedule, I offered them the same deal. Not one took it.

Top performers are different and should be treated as such.

## 23. Not Understanding the Relationships Between Strategy, Tactics, and Execution

Strategies are the high-level questions and answers that lead you to move in the direction that you choose. As a new manager, the company's strategies are set for you and, in many cases; you have little control over the strategies, even at your team level. But sometimes you *do* have control. D-Day resulted in a strategic decision to settle the European war before the Pacific. Once that strategic decision was made, the tactics of a successful invasion became paramount. On a smaller scale, you, as a leader, will be making some of the same higher-level strategic decisions and many precise and detailed tactical decisions.

Then comes execution. Some have said that a strategy poorly executed was never a good strategy. Certainly, a poor strategy well executed is not optimal either. Not long ago, I asked fully commissioned brokers to develop a business plan for the upcoming year. They set their strategy and developed their tactics; most did a great job in both areas. Where they failed was in the execution of their good plan. Once it was written and discussed, most reverted back to old habits. Keep in mind that the tactics were built around in-depth research on how certain behaviors produced significant increases in production; yet their behaviors were so ingrained that most were unable to execute a great plan.

Try reading Larry Bossidy's book *Execution: The Discipline of Getting Things Done* for more insight.

## 24. Not Understanding the Critical Issues Affecting Performance and Not Ensuring That Your Team Understands Them As Well

The majority of your team members (and the majority of employees in your company) do not understand the factors impacting their (and yours) industry and company. The majority seldom read an industry journal. In fact, I once heard that only about 50 percent of Americans have read a book in the past year. If that is true, how can you assume that your employees have read or listened enough to understand the factors that are impacting their business? Add to this Gallup's research into engaged and disengaged employees, and you have the majority of employees who do not understand the external or internal factors influencing the success or failure of the company and themselves.

It is imperative that you understand, through discussion, reading, and asking a lot of questions, what the critical issues are that impact your business and the success of your employees.

If you were an investment advisor in 2011, the impact of the poor economy is easy to see and understand. But, if you are in your thirties or forties and plan to be in the same profession for twenty more years, you need to know what the impact of the regulators' focus on suitability will be, what the impact on your career of upcoming regulations dealing with fiduciary responsibility will be, how insurance companies will react to the regulators' increasingly negative view toward variable annuities, and how another two years of low interest rate will affect you and your performance. Shouldn't every investment advisor be asking these questions? Shouldn't their companies be asking the same questions and having those discussions with the employees?

By the way, most of your peers, with whom you are competing, don't have any idea either!

## 25. Thinking That Members of the Team Are Concerned about Your Success

It's time to face an important fact: your team members do not care about your success. I understand that you want to believe that your team is behind you and wants you to succeed. They may like you, but your success is way down on their list of priorities.

Face that fact.

It is true that most members of a team want to be a member of a winning team; they like the accolades that result in teams being recognized, and they of course love the incentives that go along with winning. But, they have no vested interest in you winning.

Here's an example with high school baseball players. The home team is winning, it is the bottom of the fifth inning, and the clouds are getting darker. The rules state if the game completes inning six and is called due to weather, it is a complete game. If the game is called before the end of the sixth inning, it is an incomplete game and must be postponed and then completed at a later date.

Up to bat are the three top hitters on the team; it is now the bottom of the sixth inning. The coach brings the three together, explains the rules, points out that the team is ahead, and explains that if the three batters strike out, the game is over, and the team wins.

Even though the players like the coach, and even though the coach is managing an undefeated season, not one of those players could bring himself to intentionally strike out! Not one.

If a coach cannot get high school ball players to perform so that the team and the coach can be successful, how can a manager labor under the misbelief that every team member is dedicated to ensuring that the manager wins? This does not mean that they are not good people, but, if the manager believes that the team is dedicated to his or her success, the manager does not understand human behavior.

## 26. Not Using Data to Manage

Two quick stories will make the point that, as a new manager, you need to use data to help you manage. There is an organization in Washington, D.C., The Business Banking Board, which does extensive research on improving the performance of bankers who deal with small businesses. One of their studies produced the phrase "time in the seat rather than time on the street," meaning that bankers with the organization who are trained and nurtured by the organization are significantly more successful than high performers hired from competing banks. Their research is thorough, statistically correct, and longitudinal. And yet, even though the data is available to senior management, I consistently sat through meetings where the head of the small business banking team stated that "we are going out to hire stars" and thus "we don't need a training program."

LPL, the largest broker dealer in the United States, has completed a great deal of research around success of investment consultants. Their research is so targeted that they are able to show what specific activities (creating a personal business plan around activities, for example) produce what amount of additional revenue. These results are not just someone's guess, but rather, they are statistically reliable data. So why is it that the individual consultants do *not* use this data to improve performance? Why is it that an advisor who, after analyzing her performance for the previous two years and determining that she needed four appointments a day to make the income that she desired, failed to create that number of appointments for the first ten months of the year?

Data which has been determined to be reliable and valid is your friend. It can be used to improve performance. Unfortunately, most managers rely on their "gut" and on their experience to drive their behavior, even though there is no evidence that their "gut" is accurate.

The last chapter in the above story regarding the Banking Board is that, at the renewal period, only three people in the entire organization renewed their subscriptions to the reports—and not one of those three managed small business bankers. The rest, I assume, are managing using their instincts and "guts." Remember the outcome in the Amanda Knox case when the prosecutor used his gut rather than data to determine that she was guilty.

Data is your friend and your guide. Use it.

## 27. Micromanaging

In general, micromanaging individuals is a bad idea. It stifles creativity, reduces engagement by employees, and reduces the incentive for people to take risks. Asking questions, expecting answers, and holding people accountable is not micromanaging. Woodrow Wilson was known for allowing his cabinet members more freedom than any president before him—and maybe any president ever to hold office; however, the downside was his failure to understand what they were doing and the impact of what they did on his presidency and on the American public.

Micromanaging is asking for so much detail and requiring your involvement in any decision making that it impacts the efficiency and effectiveness of your employees. There will be times when you want to micromanage but, in most of your career, it is a bad idea; try to avoid it. Ask questions, give directions, express expectations, review decisions and their implications—but let your people do their jobs. If they can't do their jobs, educate them or get rid of them.

Read Howard Behar's book *It's Not About the Coffee,* and learn about letting the person who is using the broom choose the broom!

## 28. Being Too Busy or Distracted to Listen Intently

Being distracted when meeting with an employee is a clear signal that you do not respect that individual. You send that message each time it occurs. Checking e-mails, reading notes, and acting distracted gives the party with whom you are meeting a sense that you do not consider them to be important.

Here's some advice when you are meeting with an individual or your team:

- Focus on what they are saying; pay attention
- Don't check your computer; turn off the incoming e-mail notification
- Don't look at paper on your desk; look at the individual who is talking
- Acknowledge their opinions and comments
- Make them feel important

No matter what you might think of Bill Clinton, the most common attribute said of him was that "he made you feel that you were the center of the universe during your ten-second contact with him." Imagine the support you would receive from each member of your team if each one of them felt as if she or he was the center of your universe—even if only for ten seconds!

## 29. Believing That You Cannot Say, "I Don't Know"

As a new manager, there will be many times when you do not know the answer to a question you are asked. It is better to say you don't know than to give information that is incorrect. Any time a politician answers a question when he or she does not really know the answer, there is serious fallout. It is always better to say, "I don't know" than to give incorrect information.

Keep in mind that this is a short-term situation, and the timeline is much shorter than you would expect—or like. At some point, your understanding of the details and numbers associated with your team must be solid. Get in the weeds, and understand the details.

But there will be times in your continuing career when you don't know the answer to a question asked. It is *never* better to make up information or guess rather than say that you don't know.

## 30. Not Taking the Time to Hire the Right People

It has been said that it takes two weeks to hire people—and eighteen months to get rid of them if they are not the right people for the job. New managers often believe that they need to fill open positions quickly. I understand the impatience, uncertainty, and the apprehension around open positions, lost production, and budgets. However, the consequences of hiring the wrong person are dramatically more impactful on your team, your time, and your expense budget than any benefit you might receive by simply filling the position.

Every new manager (and many experienced managers) makes this mistake, so use this advice wisely. Here are some suggestions:

- Take your time. This is not emergency surgery or a life-threatening disease. You are hiring a member of your team whom you need to be a productive contributor. It is not easy, and it takes time.
- Review and investigate the applicant's background and real performance as much as you need to. It is crucial that you understand this person.
- Get your team and even your colleagues from other divisions involved in the process. Their different perspectives can be extremely helpful, and, once they suggest hiring someone, they are invested in that individual's success.
- Brian Tracy, a well-known management consultant, suggests that you interview someone three different times in three different locations so that you can get a good idea of who the individual is in different situations. Tracy also

*Management Mistakes*

states that if you would not take this individual home to have dinner with your family, do not hire the person. You can teach him or her how to do a job but you cannot teach anyone how to be nice!

- Review every resume submitted; don't let a staff person in HR tell you who is or is not qualified.
- If you have to make a choice between an inexperienced individual who is already with your team or already with the company and has a good reputation, or someone from outside the company, choose the internal candidate. It is easier to train for the job than it is to teach the culture.

## 31. Not Keeping the Team Focused on Results Regularly

Imagine coaching a football team where the team knew the score only at half-time and at the end of the game. How in the world would you motivate that team to continue fighting to win? That team would not be a competitor, and your team will not be a competitor unless you keep team members intently aware of where they are in terms of meeting their goals, and, since most companies measure internal teams against each other, against other teams.

Data is often not available or it is available on only a monthly basis. If this is the case, you need to develop a manual process for producing data and comparisons on a more regular basis. Weekly data is important and very useful as you try to motivate your team to perform at a higher level.

Some suggestions:
- Weekly reporting
- Make sure it is accurate
- Ensure that it is readable and easy to understand
- Report what is important; leave out what is not
- Go over the results with you team weekly

## 32. Not Understanding What Motivates Each Individual

Teaching helped me understand that individuals are motivated by different things. Helping kids succeed is always a challenge and it is a wonderful reward for a teacher when they do. To help students succeed, every teacher has to understand what motivates each and every student in the class. There is never one factor that motivates everyone.

Many managers believe that money is the single most important motivator and motivates everyone. There is a great deal of research, including Daniel Pink's book *Drive*, which shows that this belief is not accurate.

Years ago, I had three top performers working for me. The first, a young man with a family, was driven by money. Therefore, I found ways to reward him with money for his performance and his improvements in performance. The second was an older woman for whom money was not important—but being number one in any sales category that we tracked was her dream. She strived to be number one in everything. So, each time we tracked something in which she was first (and that was often), I sent notes, faxes, and e-mails to everyone, noting the rankings. The third individual was a quiet performer who did not like notoriety, did not like to be recognized, and, for her, money was not important. She did respond wonderfully to a note, an e-mail, or a phone call congratulating her and thanking her for her contributions. Needless to say, whenever she was at the top or had a chance to near the top, I responded with a call or a note.

It is crucial that you learn early what motivates each member of your team and that you use this knowledge to win.

## 33. Sweating the Small Stuff While Missing the Important Things

Small stuff and details are not the same thing; you need to be an expert on the details of your business. Ray Lewis, linebacker of the Baltimore Ravens, is said to review more game tape than anyone else in the NFL so that he can learn the details of the other team. Failure to understand details will show that you do not have a grasp of the business.

On the other hand, the small stuff about which you should not sweat are those things that make little difference but distract you from doing what you need to do to be successful. It might be a comment from one of your employees, something that you cannot control, or rumors. I once had an employee blow up in a meeting and refuse to record his performance around some goal, as I had requested. In thinking about how I would react, I was reminded of how a parent might react to a child throwing a tantrum, and I decided to let the individual cool down. I knew that I had the power, but this individual was a top performer, and my expectation was that he would come around. After two days, I reminded the individual of my request, and there were no issues—he did exactly what I wanted him to do.

Whenever you are confronted with what could be small stuff, ask yourself a few questions:

- What is the ultimate impact of this issue?
- Does it have an impact on my team's performance?
- Is it illegal, immoral, or discriminatory?
- Does it put the company at risk?
- Does it impact my career?
- On a scale of one to ten, how important is this issue?
- How much time should I spend on this issue?

## 34. Not Giving Your People Credit and Recognition for Every Success

At no time during your career is it acceptable not to give your team credit for the success of the team. Said another way, always give your team credit for success. Years ago, I worked with a woman who was possibly the most egocentric person with whom I have ever worked. She continually berated her teams for their performance, but when they performed well, she took credit in every senior management meeting. I don't know if senior management understood the situation, but certainly her employees understood. It did not take them long to understand how they were going to manage the situation. Since we were measured on twenty different goals, all of the employees that year met the minimum number of goals to keep their jobs. However, among all of them, as a team, they accomplished fewer than half of her goals. At the end of the year, she was terminated because of poor performance.

Give your team and the individuals who make up your team credit and acknowledgement for their successes. Here are some suggestions:

- Acknowledge successes in your team meetings.
- Whenever someone has a success, send him or her an e-mail—with a copy to your boss.
- Whenever you receive a compliment about one of your employees from a customer, make sure that your boss receives a copy of it. This does two things: it makes the employee feel important, and it gives your boss the perception that you have the best customer service in your organization. Perception is always reality!
- Over-acknowledge rather than under-acknowledge.

# Appendix B

### LESSONS LEARNED AND STORIES FROM FORTY-TWO YEARS OF MANAGING

An employee was managing a multimillion dollar lawsuit in which the company was the defendant. There was a general counsel, but he was focused on other issues. One day, the employee's boss called and left a voice mail criticizing that individual for engaging a law firm without following the established procedure. The boss had heard that information from someone! In fact, the boss's information was incorrect. The general counsel and the employee had had a conversation, agreed upon an approach, and the employee had implemented that approach. So, the boss had obtained information through someone who apparently did not know the facts, the boss did not confirm the information before picking up the phone, the criticism was left on a voice mail, the boss made no effort to ask the employee's view of the situation first before accusing, and even after the employee explained the situation and it was confirmed, the boss did not apologize for his actions.

There's a great example of what you should *not* do.

Here's what you always *should* do: confirm all facts before barging ahead, always talk to people face-to-face or over the phone (do not leave a message), listen to explanations, and apologize if you have erred.

The HR senior manager for a large company had a great future in front of him. However, he found it impossible to control his drinking at any party, and always ended up slobbering over the female employees, stumbling through the night, and making inappropriate jokes. He was transferred away from headquarters and assigned to a remote business line, where he still was, fifteen years later. No visibility, no responsibility to speak of, and no future. Why would anyone put his career at risk for a few drinks?

Working on a major project that required sixty-hour weeks, I arrived home one night to find flowers, a bottle of wine, and a dinner gift certificate for two to a local establishment. The gift had been sent to my wife by my boss as thanks for her support during this busy and crucial time. It was a wonderful gesture, and it solidified my wife's support for my working long hours much easier. Understand that the support of family is important to the success of your employees, and show your genuine appreciation to the family as well as to the employee.

A well-known CEO of a Fortune 500 company was delivering a speech in the eastern United States. For some reason, he believed that it was okay to veer from the prepared speech and make a joke about being in San Francisco and mistakenly thinking that a cross-dresser was a female employee. In the audience were more than six hundred employees from Maryland, Virginia, and Washington, D.C. No one had any idea of their personal leanings. Why would the CEO make such comments and put so much at risk? The only answer that any of us ever came to was his overwhelming arrogance, his belief that he was above any rules of decency, and a complete dissociation from reality.

An employee's husband was scheduled for major surgery, with the outcome less than a sure thing. Her supervisor organized other employees to provide meals, help with transportation, and even mow their yard. The supervisor really did care, and these efforts showed everyone that the word "team" meant more than just at work.

When Maryland National Bank was on the verge of failing in the late eighties, Frank Bramble, the new CEO, traveled around the franchise, talking honestly with every employee. In fact, he spent an amazing amount of time in front of employees, considering that his job was to try to save the company. What should a new manager learn from this? Management is about being there, in front of employees, telling the truth, being honest, addressing anxiety and challenges, and giving the employees some sense of control. The best leaders and the best generals lead from the front, not from headquarters.

Imagine the executive director of the state liquor commission being pulled over and arrested for driving under the influence! True story. If you cannot control your intake of alcohol, get help. Set an uncompromising rule of one drink whenever you are in public: one glass of wine or one mixed drink or one beer. After that, drink tonic and lime. A second drink is not worth your career.

During the bank consolidations of the nineties, one senior executive accepted a position at a cross-town institution. In the position he was leaving, he reported directly to the

*Management Mistakes*

president of the bank, no insignificant position. Instead of graciously resigning and moving on, he walked into the president's office, railed about how incompetent a leader the president was, and ended his conversation with instructions that were physically impossible for the president to follow! Less than ninety days after that incident, the bank that he had left purchased the bank to which he had just gone; very quickly, his new position was history. And his firing was conducted with the utmost brutality to ensure his public humiliation. Burning bridges and uncontrolled comments and actions never result in anything good. Unless you win the lottery and it is enough to keep you in luxury for the rest of your life, remember that losing control never is a winner for you. It will always, without a doubt, come back to haunt you.

The leader of a very large division held an offsite meeting of the entire management team. Attendance was somewhere around two hundred people. After the meeting, there was a reception with drinks and dinner with wine. The senior manager then decided that he would stay in the hotel area and continue drinking with some of the managers. That after-hours party disintegrated into a drunken mess, where a number of young women began comparing their breast sizes by pulling up their shirts—as the rest of the group stared. The senior manager became part of the group and never said anything or stopped the participants. That was a sure career-ender—for the senior manager, not the participants.

The young treasurer of a company was interrupted by the cleaning woman in his office as he was having sex with his assistant. Rather than apologize (after thirty years, hasn't the cleaning woman seen just about everything?), he decided to threaten her, using offensive racial terms.

His arrogance did not allow him to understand that the president's assistant and the cleaning woman started at the company at about the same time, their kids had grown up at the same time, and while they were of different social status, they had common bonds. The next morning, the cleaning woman sat down with the president's assistant and shared her fear over being threatened. The treasurer's career came to an abrupt end. The comedian Jeanne Robertson says, "Have you ever wanted to grab someone by the cheeks and ask 'Is there anyone home?'"

An executive vice president, after some discussion, was asked why she had made a particular decision. Her answer was, "We've already talked about that." She was unable to give a logical business reason for making a decision that had been tried in the industry, had never worked, and was opposed by most of her direct reports. If you cannot find a solid business reason for doing something, why would you do it and put your reputation and respect at risk? Arrogance!

Another executive vice president, at a dinner for board members, turned to one of her direct reports and proceeded to say, "Nobody likes her," referring to another executive. Does one's position give permission to make such statements? What value is served?

# The Final Word

As much as we wish otherwise, our children must learn from their own experiences. It seems impossible for them to take what we have to tell them and process it, so as not to make those same mistakes. But children are children, and this is not about children. It is about adults who are assuming or have assumed their first management positions. As adults, we have the opportunity to learn from others' mistakes. You've read about Jim, read the expanded mistake clarifications, and read real-life examples. Let me take this opportunity for some final words:

1. Alcohol is never your friend. There is no reason to drink at any meeting. So, here are the rules:
    a. If you are attending a corporate function, drink soda, drink tonic and lime, drink water. Over-indulging has no positive impact on your career or management's perception of you.
    b. Never ever drink and drive. Just imagine a DUI in the newspaper.
    c. If you are the individual who is responsible for a meeting, don't serve alcohol. Imagine an employee

attending the party and then killing someone on the way home. You and your company are at risk.

2. Affairs at work never have a good outcome. If you are not happy at home, deal with it—but not by having an affair at work. Your reputation will be destroyed; if the other individual is a subordinate, you are also setting yourself and your company up for a lawsuit.

3. Never listen to, tell, participate in, or laugh at a joke that is directed toward anyone, any race, any sex, or any other characteristic. As with the other two issues, there is no good outcome for you. In addition, this is another instance where you could be sued.

4. Do not talk about anyone in the company to anyone either inside or outside of the company. You never know to whom you will report in the future. If you need to complain, start a diary.

5. Never attempt to hide mistakes or issues. In every case, the cover-up or failure to be transparent is worse than the mistakes.

www.ingramcontent.com/pod-product-compliance
Lightning Source LLC
Chambersburg PA
CBHW030741180526
45163CB00003B/876